PRAISE FOR

I Swear to Tell the Tooth

"Deftly written by a dentist who clearly has a winning sense of humor."

—Dr. Geoff Jones, VA pediatrician

"Better written than a book I just edited by a best-selling author."

—Michael Garrett, Stephen King's first editor

"Amazing stories ... thoroughly enjoyed it!"

—WRWL, Amazon reviewer

"A great tribute to dentistry, family, fellowship, and life."

—Dr. Mary Alice Connor, PA dentist

"I enjoyed it very much."

—Steve Vogel, contributor to the *Washington Post*

"A handsome and witty book. A true gem ... can't wait for the sequel."

—Cynthia Armstrong, MD, RN

"Couldn't put it down!"

—Bill Rhea, underemployed Texas nice guy

D0841884

THE

WHOLE

TOOTH

OTHER BOOKS BY DR. CARROLL JAMES

I Swear to Tell the Tooth

THE
WHOLE T🦷🦷TH

More Humorous
(and Sometimes Touching)
Tales from a Globe-Trotting
Dentist's Storied Life

by

DR. CARROLL JAMES

RIDGEPUBLISHING

Published 2016

ISBN: 978-0-9967917-1-7
Library of Congress Control Number: 2016931125

Editing and book design by Stacey Aaronson

Published by:
RidgePublishing

Printed in the United States of America

This book is dedicated to the
Chinentaco Peoples of Mexico

CONTENTS

PROLOGUE

I ducked into Grandma's closet for what seemed like the hundredth time to hide from the witch, but as always, she knew I was cowering inside. She flung open the door while heckling. This time, I thought for sure I would be asphyxiated by her foul breath or devoured by her gnarly teeth or my soul would be sucked out and hurled down into Sheol.

I suddenly awoke, jerked wide awake by sheer night terror. I was lying in a puddle of sweat-soaked bed sheets, happy that I again escaped her clutches—a fate I had been convinced throughout my childhood would be worse than death. I began to jump on my bed, bouncing and laughing with relieved abandon, not caring who in my own house might hear. I was about twelve.

Suddenly, my bedroom door flew open. In the darkness, I caught the faint outline of a pointed hat, its sagging, wrinkled peak pointing spear-like at me. I tried to yell for help but no sound would come. The witch, with her bad breath, decayed teeth, and lolling knotted tongue stepped through the door, approaching with more deliberate determination than she ever had within Grandma's farmhouse. As she closed in on me, a sinister leer crinkled her green-hued face. She cackled softly before emitting an earsplitting shriek. The end was near. This was it; the dream had become a reality.

When she pressed her worm-ridden body against the bed, the room became swirling-surreal and I awoke for a second time. My heart was pounding and I was sweat-soaked like never before. Not trusting my senses—was I really awake?—I got up and tiptoed over to the still-closed bedroom door, which wasn't latched. I cautiously pushed it. As it opened, a creak made me gasp. There was no one in the hall, but I was afraid the thumping in my chest might attract the attention of that witch.

My parents and brother were asleep in their rooms. Dad was snoring, which tonight, and only tonight, was a welcome sound. There was no late-night TV in the fifties; the National Anthem had already been played on all three stations, so I shuffled into the family room and looked for something to read. I found a Hardy Boys mystery and switched on the light of a gooseneck lamp, but not before locking all the doors. (We seldom locked our doors in my childhood home in Potomac, MD. Grandma's farmhouse in Southwest Virginia didn't even have locks.)

The dream followed me far into adulthood, but as I grew older it faded to less frequent until it eventually stopped altogether. I still read late into the night, however. A habit? A defense? It's late right now, and my wife Kate is sleeping soundly. She falls asleep before her head hits the pillow. It's a gift.

My own modus operandi could also be viewed as a gift. I accomplished a lot in the middle of the night while growing up. That's how I got through dental school. I simply had more hours in my day than most people.

As I relate this, I am tired yet still restless. Sleep is not an immediate option, so I scan my library. I've been reading William L. Shirer's monumental work *The Rise and Fall of the Third Reich*, but the evil that emanates from those pages might attract the witch, and I don't want to give her an opening into my world. I look for something lighter and spot Robert Fulghum's *All I Really Need to Know I Learned in Kindergarten*, but that's too much fun. *I'll probably be up all night*, I think.

On my desk beside my computer is a technical journal from The Academy of General Dentistry. I take an Ambien, which has the effect of red wine coupled with a thick steak, and open the magazine to an article: "Osteoclastic Activity in Mandibular Ameloblastomas." *That ought to do it.* The back of my eyelids await.

In a fog, I find myself groping down our hallway to the master bedroom. Keeping that witch in the background, at arm's length, is the best I can hope for. I pull the covers up and drift off. *Tomorrow, I'll start working on my next book and ...*

———

CHAPTER ONE

102 Years

K ate and I initially met many of our widespread neighbors at the small country church in Gloyd. Perched on the crest of a gentle rise, Gloyd's picturesque clapboard church seems to leap from a Norman Rockwell painting. The arched doorway stretches toward a bell tower, atop which a tall steeple beckons all in need of heavenly solace. An ancient graveyard, planted before the church was built in 1879, lies softly on the rolling hillside out back.

The Presbyter was the community's anchor, its pastor the unofficial town mayor. Alongside the Gloyd Civic Association, Pastor Winston was the real guiding force for over forty years. Community meetings and social gatherings took place in an all-purpose building down the hill, while the Gloyd Federal Credit Union was housed in a closet-sized room in the basement and run by the church treasurer, Charlie, who sported a Santa beard, overalls, and in wintertime, the same lightweight sweatshirt regardless of the temperature. Hours were Tuesday and Thursday evenings between five and seven, and Saturday morning between nine and one, or whenever Charlie was around. If the customer needed cash, Charlie might open his weather-beaten wallet. "I've got $27. Will that hold you over?" The credit union had a wooden desk with a drawer full of handwritten IOUs to Charlie.

At Christmastime, hayrides ended with hot cocoa at the church; a gently falling snow sometimes complemented the outings. The Girl Scouts, the American Legion, and AA also met in the all-purpose hall. A recent honorarium celebrated thirty-one years of faithful service by Gloyd's only postal carrier, Art.

The congregation shouldered the burden of the hall's upkeep, but Pastor Winston never turned down a donation because utilities like electric and Internet charged the church steep business rates—they cut into funds that would otherwise be available for service programs, soup kitchens, battered women, addictions, clothing drives, etc.

When Kate and I first joined, the tight-knit congregation was comprised mostly of old-timers. Twenty-five years down the road, the James clan was warmly accepted, although still considered newcomers.

One or two families of color occasionally worshiped in the Presbyter on Sunday, but most attended the traditional black Methodist church a mile down the road. Pastor Winston, a Pittsburg transplant, sponsored a few interdenominational functions—picnics, sunrise services, sports, etc.—but these were seldom successful. The old-timers, black and white, were comfortable with the established distinctions. I never overheard racial slurs or distasteful jokes, but looks can be deceiving.

In an era when racial barriers were breaking down, particularly in the South, such attitudes seemed incongruous and at odds with biblical principles. It's been said, "The most segregated hour in Christian America is on Sunday morning." Only after many years since Kate and I moved to Gloyd have we seen this slowly change.

Although job opportunities were quite different for blacks and whites, both had grown up playing horseshoes and mumblety-peg, and meeting at the fishing hole on a lazy summer afternoon. But on Sunday they attended separate churches, worshiping God in superficially dissimilar ways. It seems weird today, but true transformation is of the heart; I don't think many of the older pew-warmers even recognize how radical the change has been.

One elderly black couple, Tom Simpson and his lovely wife Selma, were fascinating folks with a remarkable family history. Their parents were college graduates at a time when most white people, my father included, didn't have a high school diploma. Thus two of the most highly educated people in Gloyd at the turn of the twentieth century were black. Tom and Selma left the area to attend college like their parents and developed successful professional careers.

In Chicago, Tom was a private investigator for a prestigious law firm; the scar above his left eyebrow testified to exciting exploits. Selma became established in the art world, selling hundreds of her brilliant watercolors. She carried herself well, more refined than Tom who, despite his education, remained a good ol' boy at heart. When they returned home to old friends and a well-deserved retirement, they alternated between attending the black church and the white church on any given Sunday. Born and raised in Gloyd, they were welcomed by both congregations.

As our farmette backed up to the remnants of Tom's ancestral dairy farm, he and I occasionally chatted over the fence. But although he was a good neighbor, he was never a close friend. In fact, Kate and I forever remained outsiders.

Selma's ancestors were born into involuntary servitude— the horrors of slavery by a more genteel name. Many had braved the dangerous trek from Maryland to Canada via the Underground Railroad. A hundred and twenty years later,

Tom and Selma hosted a family reunion one summer that was featured in *The Washington Post*. Thirty or so Canadian kinfolk returned to become reacquainted with their American cousins.

Through my participation in US-USSR Bridges for Peace, I had become friendly with a Pastor Steve of a socially progressive denomination in the nearby suburbs. The lily-white congregation espoused helping the poor and reaching out to people of color but there was little real action.

One cheerful Sunday afternoon Pastor Steve and his wife drove out to pay us a visit. While we chatted over Kate's delicious apple pie, there was a knock on the back door. It was Tom, which was highly unusual because we typically only talked over the fence.

"Hey, everybody—this is our neighbor, Tom," I smiled.

A man of few words, Tom said, "Howdy, ya'll."

Making no allowance for the Lord's Day, he wore his usual: a battered straw hat, threadbare overalls with patched knees, a faded plaid shirt, and well-worn work boots covered in muck. A sprig of straw dangled from his mouth. Selma probably didn't know he was calling on us. She would've been horrified.

"How about some dessert, Tom?" I asked.

"Yep. That pie sure looks good."

Everyone retired to comfortable chairs in our sunroom where Tom jawed, often on indelicate subjects. "I tell ya how we castrated a horse in them ole days …" Even Selma hadn't been able to take the country out of him. During a lull, Tom leaned sideways and raised his butt to retrieve a soiled handkerchief from his back pocket. He blew—loudly—then inspected the rag, carefully refolded it, and stuffed it back into his overalls.

Shifting uncomfortably, Pastor Steve's wife pretended not to notice. I smiled because I at first thought he was going to pass gas. Tom was pretty old.

"Got to git. Thanks for the pie, Kate. Good meeting ya'll." Tom struggled to his feet, then limped through the kitchen and out the back door. His gimpy left leg complemented the glass eye on his right side, which rolled erratically, reminding me a little of Ole Lincum, the black sharecropper who taught me to play mumblety-peg near my grandmother's home on Nealy Ridge.

After the screen door banged shut behind him, silence filled the room. Our guests wore frozen smiles and commented on how "quaint" he was.

"He seemed comfortable inside your home," Steve said. I knew what was implied—in the home of *white* folk.

Trying to hide my indignation, I politely said, "That old coot and his beautiful wife are two of Gloyd's most highly educated, accomplished, and respected residents."

Pastor Steve's jaw dropped (Tom would've called it slack-jawed). He and his wife had assumed that this bent, crippled old black guy was another sad byproduct of the Old South.

I later regretted suggesting that they "not judge a book by its cover"; I hadn't meant to be mean-spirited. Later that night, during quiet reflection, I thought, *Actually, Tom is quaint.* But I liked to think of him as a "character."

I had recently hung out the shingle on my rural office when Tom ambled over one fine spring morning—without an appointment. He loudly demanded, "I've got a tooth that needs pulling, right now. It's been painin' me awhile." Like many of his generation, he wasn't the least bit interested in "spending a lot of money on one that's about had it."

"Come on in, Tom. Give me a minute to open up and I'll have a look-see."

While I flipped the lights on and fired up the compressor, he sat in the dental chair. Despite the broken one, most of his pearly whites were in pretty good shape. I easily removed the offending tooth and Tom was happy. "Don't forget my senior citizen's discount," he reminded me, peeling off the exact amount from a wad of grungy bills he kept stuffed deep inside his overalls.

A year later Tom called our home phone, again bypassing a formal appointment as if the business phone didn't exist.

"You've gotta come over and check out my mother-in-law. It's urgent, Doc."

Selma's mother must be older than Methuselah, I thought. She lived with them and had recently developed a serious toothache. If I didn't know better, I would've said he sounded flustered, but Tom didn't get flustered, and she'd had this pain for a while, so it didn't seem urgent to me, and I'd had a hard day.

"Bring her in tomorrow morning, Tom. I'll be glad to take a look."

"I *told* you. She can't be moved," Tom shouted into the phone.

I guess I missed that part. "So, exactly what's wrong?"

"Ain't you been listening? She's not eaten in days and now won't drink anything."

Now that did sound serious, more than a panicky son-in-law. "Okay, Tom. I'll be over this evening, as soon as we close up here."

"Great." He hung up the phone with no wasted words.

I muttered good-bye to a dial tone while wondering what I'd gotten myself into. Kate, however, was excited about a house call, which is not something a dentist often does. My helpmate packed up a few essentials: mirror, explorer, periodontal probe, gauze, and latex gloves.

At dusk, we arrived at Tom's ranch house, greeted by a pack of growling silhouettes. In the descending blackness, they sounded ominous. Although I'd mostly gotten over it, I had become skittish around unleashed, barking dogs during my college summers as a mailman—memories of numerous attacks during deliveries kept me from feeling the least bit ashamed about running from them.

Tom's screen door creaked open and the growling intensified. A deep baritone shouted, "Ge'-on-out-o'-'ere!" I quickly turned to run, but then realized he was talking to the dogs, not us. In a calmer tone he reassured, "Their bark is worse 'n their bite. Come on in."

So they do in fact bite? My heart raced.

Selma flipped on the porch light, which not only highlighted her warm smile, but prompted me to bolt toward the open door, leaving Kate in the dust. Unflustered, Kate bent over and made fast friends with the first dog that approached. At her gentle touch, the whole brood began wagging their tails, licking her hands and nuzzling.

Kate and I had never been inside the Simpsons' home, so it was the first time we'd seen Selma's art. Her watercolors, along with family photographs, adorned their walls: myriad country scenes of farmhouses; faded red barns emblazoned with *Chew Mail Pouch Tobacco*; fields of corn, hay, and sorghum; draft horses straining against ploughs, reapers, or wagons; grazing cows; farmers sowing and reaping; family picnics on a Sunday afternoon; and children swaying on a tire swing, all based on personal experiences in bygone pastoral Gloyd.

While admiring these lovely paintings, I was reminded of a story I'd heard about an altercation between Tom and the county assayer.

Perched on a rolling hill, Tom and Selma's home overlooked a deep-blue lake. Along the base of this slope, the wandering shoreline greeted gently lapping waves as cattails swayed to and fro, but Tom and Selma didn't enjoy the serenity.

Washington DC's increasing water demands had required a new reservoir, which took a substantial slice of the countryside, including most of what had once been Tom's dairy farm. Along with other affected farmers, he fought valiantly to forestall the appropriation of his birthright, but city hall ultimately won, leaving about thirty-five acres of high ground, upon which the retired couple built a new home. Tom's ancestral farmhouse was underwater.

The county dramatically increased their real estate assessment because Tom and Selma's rump acreage had become prime lakefront property. After the "theft" of his childhood home, Tom was livid about the augmented tax. He doggedly appealed through one formal hearing after another until finally, the county dispatched a special agent to his house to mollify Tom, whom they believed was no more than an old country bumpkin.

A dust-covered, government-issued compact arrived at the ranch house one hot, stagnant summer afternoon. The unsuspecting city boy driving it had not the slightest clue what he was in for. Tom stormed out of his house surrounded by barking dogs, wearing his bibbed overalls fastened on only one side to reveal a torn T-shirt, his ragged straw hat capping the rage on his wizened face. He hovered so close to the door that the driver couldn't open it.

The inspector rolled down his window and peered up at him. Tom's jaw was firmly set, his neck veins popping and fists tightly clenched, an attack dog waiting for the go-ahead. The taxman, dressed in an ill-fitting polyester suit, nervously eyed the snarling mutts circling his car that although ready to pounce, stood down at their master's command.

Tom then stepped aside, allowing the poor guy to climb out. Standing and straightening his rayon tie, he noticed the placid lake brimming with ducks, geese, swans, and herons, and a sailboat gliding across the backdrop of a pine-green forest.

With renewed confidence, the assayer said, "What a lovely setting. You're a lucky man."

At this the watchdogs growled low; they knew Tom's body language. He exploded, cutting the man short with a string of expletives not fit to print, then grabbed the young man's arm and escorted him into his house. The dogs closely followed as they entered the living room, where Tom proudly showed him Selma's paintings, giving the assayer time to breathe calmly. Tom related the history of each and every scene painted during those pleasant years preceding the "acquisition" and subsequent flooding of his family farm, including the farmhouse in which he was raised.

The official stammered, "These ... these are all *very* lovely. Your wife is obviously talented. But what can this possibly have to do with your tax rate?"

Straightening up tall, Tom thundered, "They're all pastoral scenes. Do you see any nautical crap on my walls?" The dogs leaned in. "That damn lake covered the memories of my youth, lovingly captured and preserved on canvas by Selma." The country lingo was gone as the legal detective in him took over.

The taxman knew defeat and wrote a favorable report. Tom won the case, and his assessment has never been increased.

Kate and I were now surrounded by this same gallery in Tom and Selma's home.

"Who wants some homemade cookies and lemonade?" Selma asked, walking in with a tray.

Though our purpose wasn't a leisurely visit, we sat on her Victorian couch to sample her baking, which was as good as her art. Afterward, Tom escorted us down a narrow hallway. His gimpy stride led us past an art room cluttered with easels, canvases, pallets, brushes, rags, and half-squeezed tubes. I wanted to stop and see what Selma was currently working on, but Tom continued to a small guest room at the far end.

As I stepped into the sickroom, I had to stifle a gasp. Tom's mother-in-law lay face up on a hospital bed, frail and wrinkled, moving nary a muscle in response to our intrusion. Looking closely, I could detect no breathing, no movement of her chest. The stainless-steel rails were locked in place as if she might attempt an escape, though there was little chance of that. Gracefully folded over her breast, her shriveled hands suggested an eerie sense of peace—maybe a little too much so. The funereal vision would've been complete if a lily had been inserted between her arthritic fingers.

I'm just a dentist, for crying out loud! I looked at my watch. *Let's see ... time of death—7:12 PM.* I was beginning to lose it.

Desperately, I searched Kate's face and silently mouthed, What now? Her perplexed expression mirrored my own confusion; no help there. I then made eye contact with Tom, who had gone around to the far side of the bed. With his large rough hands, he quietly gestured that I should come closer.

I took a deep breath and stepped up to the bedside. It was time to take charge. Kate unwrapped our small bundle of instruments on the decorative linen covering a dresser.

"It's been days since she's eaten anything and now refuses water," Tom muttered.

That's not good. I then noticed her chest ever so slightly rise and fall, the rhythm barely discernible. *So ... she's not dead.* However, lethal dehydration was a pressing issue.

Tom leaned across the bed and whispered, "She might not want to open." She looked pretty weak, so I gently teased her dry lips with my gloved hands. More determined, I further prodded, which only prompted her to firmly purse as a child might.

"Come on, sweetie. Open up so I can have a look." When I tried to force her jaw open, she suddenly sprang to life, vigorously shaking her head from side to side. *Well ... at least there's some life left in the old gal.* She wasn't going to die on us in the next few minutes.

I looked up at Tom who gazed back, almost reserved. I had never imagined Tom with a gentle side. Tenderly he mouthed, Mother's a bit hard of hearing.

Almost reverently, he bent over to persuade her to cooperate with the nice dentist, his lips nearly touching her ear. I half expected him to kiss her. But without warning, his neck veins bulged and in a deep, gravelly voice he shouted, "MOTHER! THE DENTIST IS HERE!"

Startled, I tripped backwards and crashed into Kate, who lost her balance, fell against the wall, and knocked into one of Selma's paintings, which plummeted to the floor. It was a portrait of Mother.

Kate bent down and snatched up the family treasure, all the while stifling an outburst of laughter that begged for release. She sported that same impish look when she once accidentally splattered ink all over me and my office. Mortified, I stared at Tom, who was looking at Kate wide-eyed. He then turned and looked at me with an ever-so-slight grin.

In the end, Tom's sonorous pronouncement worked—his mother-in-law opened wide. I was surprised to find that all of her teeth were present, unlike Tom's, and in relatively good condition with the sole exception of the offending one, which was so badly decayed and infected that it needed to be extracted.

I telephoned a respected oral surgeon, who was a good friend, at his home, telling him the condition was pretty serious, that the tooth was abscessed and needed to come out.

"I'll be right over, Carroll."

"Thanks. And don't worry about the dogs."

"Uh, what dogs?"

"They're harmless enough—I think. I'll wait for you inside."

A half hour later, the barking announced Doug's arrival and Tom went outside to save him.

I watched in silent amusement as my friend entered the bedroom and stopped short. He shook his head. "This needs to be done in a hospital."

Good call. After all, Selma's mother was one hundred and two years old, dehydrated, and uncooperative.

Believe it or not, this woman I initially took for dead was

back home a couple days later, up and about, eating and drinking normally. Another satisfied customer!

Doug the surgeon enjoyed coming to Gloyd so much that he and his family built a home there. He eventually opened an office just down the road from the country store where the train had derailed years earlier, spilling new Cadillacs everywhere (see *I Swear to Tell the Tooth* for that story). His surgical practice immediately began to thrive, helping Gloyd to enter the modern world.

Early on a crisp fall morning, a couple months after my house call, I noticed Tom strolling through the back field with that perpetual sprig of straw dangling from his mouth. He saw me walk toward the fence and wandered over for a friendly chat. Not an hour before, as dawn broke over the Sunday countryside, several hot-air balloons had lifted from a nearby field.

On nice weekends these floating apparitions prompted a plethora of dogs, including mine, to howl and yelp with joyous abandon. Kate and I would head outside in our bathrobes to enjoy a cup of coffee while watching the balloons ascend in poetic tandem with the rising sun. As many as a dozen could be seen dotting the skyline.

Leaning against a fence post with one foot propped on the bottom rail, I said, "Aren't those colorful balloons regal?"

Big mistake!

Tom's eyes narrowed. "I can't stand those damn things. They get my dogs to barkin' loud enough to wake the dead. They only shut up once I'm out of bed." Tom kicked a clod of dirt. "They're invadin' my airspace. Next time one comes over my property, I'm gittin' my shotgun and groundin' it!"

In my head: *Well ... nice talking with you Tom.* Out loud: "Geez ... well ... just look at the time. Gotta get ready for church. Don't wanna be late."

I dashed toward my house but paused to call back to Tom. "By the way, how's your mother-in-law doing?"

He stopped, turned around, and grumbled, "Her? Oh … she'll live."

Yep, definitely time for church.

Age finally caught up with Tom and Selma, and they eventually moved back to Chicago where their kids had found a retirement home for them. One daughter drove a U-Haul north after packing their few personal effects while Tom and Selma planned to fly out. She insisted that Tom not wear overalls on the plane, being of the old school that dictated dress clothes when traveling by air. So she dusted off a pair of Tom's black penny loafers, ironed a pair of polyester pants along with a dress shirt, and retrieved his old sports jacket from the hall closet, a coat that hadn't seen the light of day in decades.

"Everything's too tight," he grumbled. Selma thought he looked sharp and smiled.

He frowned and complained as they walked through the airport and stepped through the metal detector. When the buzzers went off, TSA agents went into action.

"Is this your jacket, sir?"

"Yeah. Why?" Tom tried to look menacing, but he'd become stooped with age and couldn't quite pull it off. He glared at Selma. "I told you I shouldn't have worn this damn thing."

Although polite, post-911 TSA inspectors can be firm. "Step over here, sir. Please empty all your pockets into this container."

It took Tom a while to fumble through his pants and display the contents.

"Sir. You can't take a knife on board. And what's this? A lighter?"

"That's my Zippo. An' I always carry a pocketknife. Give 'em back, you little twerp!"

About that time, the X-ray tech shouted, "Hey, Lou. Check this out."

After glancing at the screen, two inspectors began riffling through Tom's coat pockets.

"Here's a shotgun shell," the first one shouted.

"There's another one in this pocket," the second inspector said. "And another one. He has three loaded shells!"

With an agent grasping each arm, Tom was escorted to a small room where he continued to loudly complain. He was fit to be tied and the agents almost had to do just that.

"I don't even own a shotgun anymore. Sold the last one to Luke. Been years now. What the hell do you think I'm gonna do with old shells and no gun?"

Selma, ever the voice of reason, came to his rescue. She explained that this gruff old man, "unfortunately my husband," hadn't worn the coat for years and had no clue that shotgun shells were in the pockets. She agreed to pay shipping for the Zippo and penknife if they'd just let him get on the plane. Her soft, classy demeanor was disarming, and the chief inspector, who'd been called in, finally acquiesced, probably happy to be rid of the old coot.

But Gloyd wasn't happy to be rid of him. Folks missed them. I know I did. I've tried to imagine Tom shooting pheasants in a sports jacket, but I doubt if he ever felt compelled to wear one again.

CHAPTER TWO

Irene

"They hung up on me," Irene, my new receptionist declared. "That's three times today."

After several loyal years on the job, Natalia, my previous receptionist, had moved to the beach in Delaware. I moped around the office all day when she gave notice. "How can I keep track of the TV soap operas?" I had said with a sheepish grin.

"You won't," she had replied.

Our son Joel was still a toddler and Kate wasn't ready to work full-time, so she could only fill in at reception part-time; my trustworthy assistant, Louise, did double-duty when Kate wasn't there. This arrangement couldn't last long term, so I was desperate to find a full-time receptionist who could make things run smoothly, especially with two offices, one in a modern medical building in Rockville and the other attached to my country home in Gloyd.

One day, a friend told me about his neighbor who was looking for an administrative job in the medical field. She not only came highly recommended with a great resume, but her own kids were older now and in school all day—the same situation I'd found with Louise—and that had worked out great.

When me met, Irene made quite an impression. Her short brown hair, uneven across the back as if she'd cut it herself, accentuated her round face. With closely trimmed, unpainted fingernails and a necklace of faux pearls draped over a sack dress of large print flowers, she was the exact opposite of Prada-perfect Natalia. She sported a huge, plastic watch on her left wrist, which I later noticed was one of several she owned in different colors—maybe purchased by the gross? A chain attached to her thick black glasses dangled over the back of her neck, giving her a studious appearance. The ensemble was finished with flats over tan socks. She could have been the model for *American Gothic* if not for the twinkle in her big round eyes and her broad grin.

During the interview, Irene's sense of humor shined, an important attribute in our office. Although she had never worked in a medical setting, she was personable with an accounting background, both assets at the front desk. As had become my habit, I hired her on the spot.

Irene exuded a gentle aura of which the patients, staff, and I soon grew fond; she was perfect for a dental office full of nervous folks. Loyal and conscientious, always arriving on time and never cutting out before five o'clock, she was quite a change from ever-tardy Natalia, who always beat the last patient out the door in the evening. Like Natalia, however, Irene could be implicitly trusted with finances. I've been grateful that despite my impulsive hiring practices, I've never been embezzled.

But in spite of the positives, there always seemed to be some unforeseen snag with Irene. She was flighty. The porch light wasn't always on, and when it was, it flickered. Forget *American Gothic*—Irene could've been a poster girl for the ditzy yet lovable receptionist.

From day one, her phone persona was pleasant. "Hello. I'm Irene. I'm *new*."

Kate suggested that she might mention the name of the office.

"I'm so sorry," she said. "How about this? 'Hello. Dr. James's office. I'm Irene. I'm new.'"

"Much better," Kate encouraged.

Like a black lab, Irene wanted to please. But ten months later, she still greeted patients with this same salutation.

"Irene," I tactfully explained, "you've been here going on a year now. You are no longer *new*. You might want to drop that."

The porch light grew bright as she tilted her head to one side and uttered her go-to response when something sank in, a soft, "Ahhh ..." It still took a couple more months, however, before she stopped telling people she was new. The habit was hard to kick.

Despite her cheerful telephone etiquette, she became flustered when the second line rang. "Hold please," she'd pleasantly announce while hitting the wrong button. Her smile would fade when she tried to reconnect with the first person by hanging up on the second one. "I don't understand why people are so rude," she'd say with a grimace.

Kate was incredibly patient with her. "Watch me, Irene. Push the hold button *before* you answer line two."

"That's what I'm doing," Irene insisted. She demonstrated by whacking it before hitting hold.

"Take it slow to make sure you don't hang up first," Kate suggested.

"I see," Irene muttered, but she didn't; the porch light dimmed. "I think something's wrong with these phones," she persisted. The porch light seemed to go completely out.

Irene considered the problem from all angles and decided to purchase a super-long receiver cord from Radio Shack, one that stretched across the business office. With that in place, she could retrieve charts, ledgers, and insurance forms without having to put anyone on hold. Clenching various papers with the receiver firmly pressed against her cheek, she'd triumphantly announce, "I've got your chart right here, Mr. Jones. Now let me get your insurance info." She'd then spin around in her rolling chair to trek farther afield, wrapping herself in the cord. Irene and her wheeled chariot regularly swept through the office while the phone cord knocked files, pencils, and coffee cups off her desk. *She's gonna choke herself to death,* I thought. Fearful of being clothes-lined in her vinyl web, I avoided her domain.

As Kate had a tendency to do, Irene tripped into walls that "miraculously jumped" at her and spilled water glasses invariably filled to the brim. Actually, she was far more klutzy than Kate.

One day, while treating my staff to lunch at a nice restaurant, I glanced at my watch and noticed it was getting late. "We'd better fly," I said.

Irene, engrossed in a story she was telling, suddenly realized we were leaving and quickly scooted to the edge of the booth. Only she went too far. Dropping out of sight, she landed on her butt with a deep thud that resonated through the restaurant. Someone else might have been embarrassed, but Irene rose phoenix-like with a good-natured grin on her face. While arranging her disheveled dress, she declared, "I can't believe I did that!" Irene was a good sport, and we all had a good laugh.

But being lighthearted in moments of humiliation, though admirable, didn't make up for the areas that were lacking. When I tried to teach Irene basic assisting, for example, in case someone was out sick or we were overly busy, her didactic skills were on par with Ms. Jacob, my klutzy classmate from dental school (who is, regrettably, Dr. Jacob now). In short, Irene could not be trusted with sharp instruments. What's more, she was adept at breaking expensive dental equipment. Upon hearing yet another crash, I could only wonder, *What's she destroyed now?* I decided to keep her away from the caustic chemicals used for sterilization—for her own safety, of course.

I had also never seen anyone for whom seating a patient could turn into an ordeal. She once nearly strangled an elderly woman after putting the chain around her neck as well as the headrest. When it caught on Irene's sleeve button as she turned to leave, I heard the patient gagging. Despite trying to make up for it I with a kind-hearted smile that exuded sincerity, I opted to keep her away from the dental chair after that. I would joke to my staff, "As long as you stay away from her phone cord, you're safe," but I knew that wasn't true.

One afternoon, our newly hired Lebanese assistant, Trish, offered to take Irene out to lunch, just the two of them.

"Sounds good," Irene said. "But if you insist on treating, I'll drive."

When they returned, Trish was shaking uncontrollably, her olive skin now pale. In contrast, Irene was all smiles as she burst through the lab door. "She hardly touched her meal," Irene announced, "so I grabbed it as carry-out." Right then she dropped the Styrofoam box, scattering Trish's half-eaten Reuben across the lab floor.

I had noticed that although Trish was petite like Natalia, she could devour a large meal, so it wasn't like her to bring leftovers back. Trish pulled me aside and whispered, "That lady's nuts. She drives like a crazy person." I smiled and suggested that it couldn't have been all that bad, but Trish never again rode in a car with Irene.

I understood why when I once ran out of gas and called the office for a ride. Irene came to the rescue, if you can call it that. After picking me up, she tore down Rockville Pike, swerving recklessly through bumper-to-bumper traffic. White knuckled, I hung on to the arm rest. She looked over at me and said, "Patients are pretty upset that you're late. But I'll get you back quickly." She almost sideswiped a truck while her eyes were off the road.

"You know, Irene, you have quite a ... a reputation behind the wheel," I stammered.

Squeezing between two produce trucks, she calmly proclaimed, "I'm driving a little slower, just for your sake."

Irene was a pit bull behind the wheel. Like Trish, I never again rode with her.

This road-trip-from-hell confirmed my decision to steer Irene away from clinical duties altogether. Despite that, she'd latch onto a new treatment modality like a teenager with the latest fad. It didn't matter if it made sense to anyone else. As long as it made sense to her, she was convinced everyone should try it.

I knew an audiologist who treated chronic headaches and upper-back pain—which can be related to grinding of the teeth—with a new biofeedback therapy. TMJ, a malfunction of the jaw joints, can be so severe that it becomes hard for the patient to chew. Biofeedback had mixed results, but my friend's new holistic approach seemed to have promise, designed to address a wide range of trigger points.

Although I'd never found any evidence of TMJ dysfunction in Irene, she was plagued with frequent headaches. I mentioned it to my audiologist friend, and he graciously offered to treat her free of charge. If it worked—great! If not, nothing was lost but time.

For her first visit, Irene left late. "I'll eat my sandwich in the car," she announced while flying through the lab door. I'm sure she hit Rockville Pike at warp speed. When Irene returned from her appointment, she was bubbling over with excitement. In only one session, she'd managed to discover the ultimate panacea for every headache in the world.

To Irene, biofeedback, coupled with a detailed list of do's and don'ts, promised to be nothing less than miraculous. My mind drifted back to years before, when we adopted our first dog, Rusty, from the animal shelter, with all the loud barking and howling—a sure-fire cure for my crippling headache would've been nice that day.

"Whatever you do, never, ever rest your chin on your hand," Irene said.

"Okay ..."

"Never rub your tense forehead."

"I guess that makes sense."

"Always use a good light for reading."

Something Mom always insisted on. "Right."

"If you think a migraine is coming on, breathe deeply and slowly exhale to fully relax."

Mind you, none of this was really new, but it was ground-breaking to Irene. What's more, anyone who didn't follow *Irene's Law* to the letter was in trouble. Case in point: Irene once caught me at my desk, chin in hand, while in profound contemplation.

"I've told you not to do that," she yelled. "It's why you get so many headaches."

Now, I'm not plagued with headaches more than the average person, but that didn't matter to Irene. I took my hand down anyway, if only to silence her.

"That's better. Now your migraine will go away," she declared triumphantly.

What happened to that gentle nature from the interview? I wondered.

"I've never had a migraine, Irene," I said.

Whoops. I'd just made a big mistake. She proceeded to yammer on for five minutes—or was it an hour?—after which I did have a headache and took a couple ibuprofen.

The next day, while casually walking past my desk, Irene again caught me red-handed. Placing her hands squarely on her hips with an air of authority, she said, "You'll never be rid of that pain if you refuse to listen to me."

In a way, she was right; her badgering gave me yet another headache. Subsequently, I kept a sharp ear for any sign of her approach, fearing she'd catch me resting my chin. When I heard her coming, I'd sit on my hands like a kid trying to hide something.

Weeks later, during a particularly busy day, my wife sidled up to Irene's reception window and unwittingly rested her chin in the curve of her hand.

"Now *you're* doing it, Kate. That's why you get headaches," Irene huffed.

Never one for undue criticism, Kate shot back, "Irene, I *never* get headaches," then promptly marched away. But she never again rested her jaw in Irene's presence. In fact, no one on staff wanted Irene to catch them in that despicable act.

One morning, Irene was uncharacteristically late. I had arrived early to work on an extensive case in the lab when I heard loud muttering drift through the door. *Did Dr. Frieden return?* (He used to have an office across the hall, and he'd mumble a lot when he wasn't lining up his golf swing.) Then I recognized Irene's distinctive ramblings.

When I heard fumbling keys, I decided to help and opened the door, which sent Irene crashing headlong into the lab while flinging an armful of stuff onto the floor. I say *stuff* because I could never figure out why she brought certain items to work every day—far more than a purse and lunch. Our lovable misfit receptionist always came prepared for a siege.

While trying to recover her treasures, she spilled the remaining bric-a-brac from her flailing arms. When I leaned over to help, our heads collided. I saw stars and once again fetched the ibuprofen.

After profusely apologizing for being late, but not for slamming me in the head—which I doubted she even noticed—she stumbled down the corridor and dumped her bounty onto the desk. Then she plopped into her chair, which surprisingly didn't roll out from under her, and breathed a sigh of relief.

Although usually late, Trish was early that day and had already activated the telephones, which upset Irene. She didn't want anyone doing her job because she was tardy. Actually, Irene was on time; she just wasn't early.

"Don't worry about it," I said. "We all get caught in traffic or something comes up. No harm done." I grinned and gave her a hug. "Just relax. Patients won't be arriving for a while."

She returned a weak smile. "I hate being late."

Irene had unwittingly picked an exceptionally full day to be so scrambled. After a cursory glance at the appointment book the previous evening, I had announced, "Tomorrow's gonna be a busy one." That meant a bag lunch for a quick bite whenever it could be fit in.

It was even busier than I'd expected, almost as bad as when Louise started working with us. Lunchtime was nonexistent, and this was the one day Irene forgot to pack a lunch, which was weird in light of all the other junk she'd lugged in. Trish shared her huge sandwich so at least our scatterbrained receptionist wouldn't starve.

At long last our workday ended and we closed up late. Everyone was eager to head out, including me. While putting my coat on, I heard Irene exclaim, "I can't believe it!"

I really didn't want to know, but trying to be a good boss, I backtracked through the lab and peeked around the corner. "What seems to be the problem, Irene?"

"My car keys are missing." She was standing slump-shouldered in the middle of her chaos.

"Do you need a ride home?" I offered, half hoping she wouldn't say yes.

"Thanks, but that's okay. I'll give Doug [her husband, not the oral surgeon] a call and have him pick me up."

"Your keys must be here somewhere," I said. "No one's gone out today. I'll help look around."

"Okay."

I remembered her grand entrance that morning. It was a good bet that her janitorial-sized key ring had slid under a cabinet or into a dark corner, but repeated searches turned up nothing. One at a time, my staff backed out the door, discretely excusing themselves.

"Gotta pick up the kids."

"I'm meeting Fred for dinner."

"If you don't need me, I'll see you tomorrow."

"We'll be fine here," I said, trying to sound upbeat while the lab door closed behind the last employee—the last except Irene.

"Did you check your bag?" The thing was more like a suitcase. "How about your coat pockets?"

"Yes, twice," she snapped, uncharacteristically short with me.

"You looked all around your office?" I asked.

She shot me a dirty look, another thing she seldom did. Suddenly she smiled, the light bulb popping on. "I know. I left them at home."

"So, Doug dropped you off this morning?"

"No. I drove myself." The light flickered.

"Well then, your keys *must* be here."

"No … ah … no. I do remember. I definitely left them at home. They're on the counter next to the refrigerator." The light dimmed.

I tried to explain that she had to have keys if she drove to work. "Did you use a spare set, a different key ring?" I remembered hearing her fumble with them that morning.

She looked up with those big brown eyes and, in a forlorn yet sweet tone, vacuously proclaimed, "I can't find my keys." The light had died, kaput. Why debate with Edith Bunker?

After further searching, during which I refrained from

asking any more questions, we found her keychain tucked behind the pencil sharpener under a pile of insurance forms she'd put there to "keep them safe."

She never quite got it that her keys had to be somewhere nearby if her car was in the parking lot. Though I looked for that slight tilt of head and the soft, telltale *Ahhhh*, it never came. Even after finding them, she clung to the idea that they were on the kitchen counter.

"Goodnight, Irene." I waved to her. "Don't forget your keys tomorrow." I smiled, hoping she'd see the humor.

She didn't. I stood in the parking lot while she sped off into the night. I'm sure she got home long before I did.

CHAPTER THREE

The Hygienist

After working with several temporaries, I finally decided to hire a permanent hygienist. Almost late for her interview, a slender young lady tripped into my private office after colliding with the doorframe. Obviously embarrassed, she extended a jittery hand and fish-gripped mine. "I'm happy ... glad ... to meet you." She looked down.

"Carro ... uh, Dr. James," Kate said (though she always tried to call me "doctor" in the office, she sometimes forgot), "I'd like to introduce Tania, the hygienist I told you about."

Tania's attire was fashionable, but not showy; her shoes were comfortable platforms, not spikes. She wore no jewelry except a wedding band tied to a rock-sized engagement ring and tiny diamonds in her ears. Her loosely bound, strawberry blonde hair framed her attractive, lightly freckled face, which had only a hint of makeup. And bonus: she wore no perfume, giving Kate another reason to immediately approve of her.

As with all interviews, I opened with a neutral icebreaker. "Hot out, isn't it?"

"Yes."

Tania's eyes shifted from the floor to the wall to the

ceiling and back to the floor while she picked at her closely trimmed and lightly glossed fingernails, so unlike the fire-engine red talons that Natalia grew.

"Tell me about your dental experience."

At that, she sat upright and became a different person. She was straightforward and bold in describing her professional skills, yet with no trace of braggadocio. Though she knocked over her Styrofoam cup and spilled coffee onto my desk (*Why would someone bring a piping hot cup of coffee to an interview?*), I somehow believed in her abilities.

Wiping up her latte, she stammered, "I ... I ... I'm sorry."

"That's okay Tania. It's fine. No harm done," I said, subtly removing the desk set that held the infamous fountain pen that Kate had once splattered all over me. Ignoring the new coffee stains on the carpet that mirrored Kate's faded ink splotches on the ceiling, I followed my instincts and hired her. Her eyes smiled with gratitude.

My gut instincts were rewarded. Her self-assurance didn't waiver, and her conscientious treatment was never tainted by mediocrity. None of my other hygienists had worked out for various reasons: not enough hours, too many hours. Another Tania, whom we loved, had moved to Alabama. A couple were classic prima donnas. But this Tania was a keeper. Esther was another story.

Esther was working for Dr. Dolph when he hired me straight out of school; when I left his practice, Rolph drastically cut her hours. A year or so later, she stopped by my new office in Minor Medical to see if I needed a hygienist. I couldn't afford one, but the trade journals said it was the next step in practice building. *One day a week won't financially kill me*, I thought.

Esther liked to talk ... and talk ... and talk, most of it about self-centered nonsense. With little tolerance for frivolities, Dr. Dolph had used my exit as an excuse to reduce her schedule. It was a good thing Irene wasn't yet working for me —she and Esther would've filled the air with nonstop, idle chatter. The big difference was that Irene had a heart of gold while Esther was self-absorbed. (In the words of Brian Regan, one of my favorite comics, "Ever been to a dinner party and one person does all the talking? Me, me, me and ... me, me, and furthermore me ...")

Though I had little contact with her, only popping into her room for my cameo patient exams, I soon realized that I'd made a colossal mistake. Esther's endless, pointless yakking put her perpetually behind schedule. Patients couldn't wait to bolt after she was finally finished with them. I began to cloister myself during lunch. She was bad for business and bad for my sanity, but how to get rid of her?

I'd yet to fire anyone and was uncomfortable with doing it. *Maybe I'll reduce her hours for "financial reasons,"* I reasoned. I prefer to avoid confrontations and therefore put it off, but when a patient called for a six-month checkup and refused to see her, I decided to cut her hours first thing the next day, despite the fact that she was already only working one day a week.

The following day Esther was late, as usual, leaving little time for niceties. "Mrs. Jones has been waiting but we need to talk first," I said, motioning to a chair in my private office. "Finances are stretched thin. I have to cut you back to every other week."

Esther's face fell. "Please, please don't," she begged. "I need the work."

"I'm sorry, but we just can't afford it." But that wasn't entirely true—my business was actually beginning to take off.

"I don't know what I'll do. My husband wants me to put in more hours, but I can't find a second job." *Maybe Mr. Esther just wants her out of the house,* I imagined.

Her juvenile pleading began to irritate. "It's the economy.

It can't be helped," I said firmly. Plus, the whining didn't help her cause.

Her face went white under the thick layer of rouge on her cheeks. Heavy-handed mascara began to trickle down and her ears flushed red. *Is that typical of a diabetic?* I became concerned and softened a tad.

"Esther, you can finish out the pay period as already booked."

Seeing a glimmer of hope that wasn't there, she left my office and seated Mrs. Jones, well behind schedule, but only after reapplying another coat of paint.

Around mid-morning, a longtime patient of mine came in for a cleaning. Joe was a big, tough guy who'd played college football as a lineman, was a corporate officer for Bechtel, and had recently returned from a tour in the Arabian oil fields. He was nice enough, but he didn't like waiting—or being yammered at. As a result, he didn't say much to Esther, which probably led her to believe that he was actually interested in her poodle's anal bleeding or her own once-a-month bloating.

Joe's appointment was about half over when he called out, "Doc!"

Natalia and I were in the operatory down the hall and didn't hear him at first over the whirr of my drill. "Doc … DOC … I need help!" That time it registered.

Hearing the urgency in Joe's voice, I told the patient to rinse and got up to duck into Esther's room. Natalia followed hard on my heels.

Next door, I found hefty Esther hunched over Joe, who was wide-eyed and struggling with her. Big Joe had a firm grip on her wrist while his legs and other arm flailed like a turtle on its back. The shock of losing her job had sent her into insulin shock. Her pupils were dilated and her sweaty face dripped globs of makeup onto Joe's forehead. She had an overall crazed look that would have scared off Freddy Krueger.

I tugged on Esther's arm, but somehow she continued scaling, her sharp rhythmic scraping digging ever deeper under Joe's gums. Blood began to trickle from one corner of his mouth. Although we pulled hard, neither Joe nor I could disengage Esther's catatonic hand.

"Natalia! We need help, now!" She ran to the other side to join the wrestling match. It took three people, two sizable men and one small woman, to muscle Esther off Joe.

As Esther sat on her stool, her hair and tunic soaked with perspiration, I told Natalia, "Get some orange juice or something sweet." Although diabetic, Esther needed sugar to restore her hormonal balance. Natalia grabbed a juice box from the frig, but Esther refused to drink, a typical reaction for a diabetic.

Natalia ran down the hall to an internist's office for professional help. His nurse came running back with several packets of sugar in hand. *Damn, I know that much.* I was hoping for some sort of injectable. "She won't take it," I practically shouted.

"You have to make her," said the calm nurse.

Looking at the razor-sharp scaler still clenched tightly in Esther's hand, I wanted to shout, *YOU force it down her throat,* but I didn't. "Okay. I'll let you know if we need anything else."

Kate took control with her composed demeanor and talked Esther into releasing the scaler, which Kate quietly placed on the bracket table. Esther finally agreed to take a few sips of juice. In the meantime Joe was standing in the corner, trying to look sympathetic but not quite pulling it off. He was clearly shaken … and looked a little angry.

"We'll cancel the morning, Esther. You go and rest in my office while we call your husband."

"This happens all the time. I'm fine to drive."

All the time! And she gets behind the wheel! I envisioned innocent pedestrians going down like bowling pins. Thankfully, her husband agreed to pick her up.

Joe rescheduled his checkup—with me. I gave him a discount.

As the years went by, Natalia moved to the shore, Irene and Louise came on board, and I went through several hygienists. Currently without one, I couldn't keep up on the recalls despite working my fingers to death. Kate bugged me to hire help and, honestly, I was just plain tired of cleaning teeth. It's tedious, backbreaking work—and those who perform this often thankless service deserve our respect and gratitude.

So that brings us back to my new hire, Tania.

With both of her boys in school, she was able to work part-time and the occasional Saturday. She always brought a change of clothes on Saturdays, which suggested she planned to meet friends for lunch or maybe shop while her husband watched the kids. (I wondered if he realized that her shift was only a half day …)

I admired how devoted Tania was as a mom; if there was an after-school activity, she asked ahead of time if she could "book off" early. She never complained about losing hours when I took a vacation or closed for a mission trip. On the flip side, if we became backlogged, she would readily tack on an extra day or two.

She was also devoted to her patients, always asking them personal questions:

"So how're the kids doing?"

"Brad must be off to college. Seems like only yesterday he was playing T-ball."

"Is your dog any better?"

"How's that new van? Packing for the beach must be easy."

Unlike Esther, who only talked about herself, Tania focused on the person in the chair. It was a mystery how she remembered so much about each individual until I saw personalized notes that she'd stuffed into their folders. Kindness and compassion came naturally to Tania. Her patients weren't merely gaping mouths.

During my initial interview with Tania, I had only one reservation about her: that she didn't drive in snow. Because she lived forty minutes away, this was a potential problem, and she admitted having a number of minor traffic accidents.

"That's okay, Tania," I said. "We've all had fender-benders."

Shades of Irene flashed before me until Tania said, "But mine were all single-car." She went on to explain. Sleet, hail, heavy rain, heavy winds, spring equinox, winter solstice, alignment of the planets, and aurora borealis all seemed to be factors.

But that didn't deter me from giving her a chance. I later told Kate about her demolition derby record.

"We'll cross that bridge when we come to it," Kate declared. "Other than that, she seems ideal." She wanted me to hire someone ... anyone.

As I gazed out the window and watched Tania accelerate much too fast down our long driveway, the smashed right front fender of her minivan caught my eye as she veered wildly from side to side.

Cities shut down in bad weather; not so in rural Gloyd (except maybe for a power outage or from the snow being too deep for anything to get through). Maryland often got its worst snows in early spring, and folks with four-wheel drives around my neighborhood couldn't wait for heavy snow—the deeper, the better.

Late on a dark Friday in March, a hard blow started and didn't let up for three days. The kids and I spent hours shoveling against the wind but finally gave up; there was no way to keep ahead of the drifting, and my small tractor wasn't up to the challenge. We brought plenty of logs inside for the wood stoves. Kate persevered longer than we did, trying to keep the garage sidewalk cleared, but she finally gave up. The last one to come inside, she forced the door closed as snow blew into the kitchen.

"I'll make hot chocolate while you take off those wet duds," I offered. "We might as well sit back and enjoy the fire, play some board games." Staring out at the swirling blizzard, I rhetorically mumbled, "No way anyone's gonna show up at the office." We hunkered down for the duration.

Tuesday arrived. The snowfall had stopped, but strong winds continued to create deep drifts. According to news reports—strangely, the electric never went down—the roads were covered several feet in places. Donning ski bibs, heavy boots, thick mittens, and a wool cap with earflaps, I trudged out to the barn to feed the horses. My son Russell's tracks from last night were obliterated, filled in by swirling snow that glittered in the bright morning sunshine. I was in the hayloft when I heard a guttural roar of a diesel engine. *Must be the train.*

After filling the mangers from above, I climbed down the horizontally challenged ladder, built by the previous owner of our farmette, Halfway Dick, and emerged into the glare of a snow-covered fairyland. One of Tania's patients, Tom the carpenter, was banging on the office door. He had struggled up the driveway in his enormous pickup truck that proudly sported a chromed vertical exhaust. It was snugly parked in the virgin snow up to its running board.

"You gotta be kidding," I exclaimed through the wool scarf, half-frozen to my beard. I gasped while trudging through the deep drifts. "Hey, Tom. We'll open up directly. Sit tight and Kate will let you in." Self-employed, Tom had no intention of missing a day's pay because of a little snow.

I took a quick shower, turned up the office heat, fired up the compressor, and sat down to clean his teeth myself. It was a sure bet that Tania wouldn't be in. Tom thanked me and hurried off to drywall someone's warm basement.

"You're okay, Doc. Tell Tania 'hi' and that I miss her."

You don't hear that about a hygienist every day.

After a year or so, Tania realized that Gloyd patients do show up for their appointments, despite the weather, so on bad days, Tania's husband dropped her off; when he traveled for business, she was a trooper and tried her best to get in on her own.

One time she got stuck a half mile away from the office, on the hill leading to the country store. Tania practically shouted through the phone, "Kate, I can't leave my car in the road. I don't know what to do."

Tania's patient, who was seated in the waiting room, overheard their conversation and volunteered to get her. "That girl is great," he said, "and so appreciated by everyone in this community."

With that, he took off in his truck to rescue her.

A warmth washed over me as I witnessed the best of humanity—kindness being returned to a good person who sincerely deserved it.

CHAPTER FOUR

Deer vs. Car

After learning to depend on Tania's expertise and judgment, she informed me that she had to take a leave of absence—her son was repeatedly hospitalized with asthma and she felt she needed to stay home with him. I ignored her two-month notice, hoping it wasn't true that she was leaving, and was consequently forced to hire a replacement at the last minute. Not surprisingly, I was desperate, and Fran was the only hygienist I interviewed who was willing to drive all the way to our Gloyd office in the country. She was also the exact opposite of Tania.

Not only was Fran always late to work, but she took an inordinate amount of time to clean a patient's teeth. She blamed my scheduling when the next person had to wait. "I'm running behind because Dr. James doesn't give me enough time to do the job properly," she would announce to the staff and any patients who were listening. "I'm the only one around here who really cares about their teeth."

This would incense me, as I cared deeply about my patients, but there was more.

A stout, stern-faced, middle-aged divorcee, Fran was a man-hater. Her disdain for me was obvious, but I was stuck with her. I couldn't fire someone, even with just cause, without being subject to steep unemployment taxes.

Our whole staff typically ate lunch around our kitchen table in Gloyd; it was a time to relax, swap stories about patients, laugh, and relate weekend plans, but Fran acted as if I wasn't in the room. Instead, she talked about her "cycle" and would berate her ex-husband, saying, "All men are plain bad." I began to hate the noon hour in my own home and stopped eating lunch with the staff.

Although I disliked confrontation, I realized that something had to be done. Toward the end of work one day, I took a deep breath and asked Fran if she could stay a few extra minutes after she was done, that we needed to talk.

"I have a hair appointment, she said. "I'll be late for it because I can't keep up with your appointment book."

"It'll only take a couple minutes," I said.

It was pushing five-thirty when we sat down in my private office. Irritated, she looked down at her watch, then glared at me.

"I'll get right to the point," I said. "A number of patients have complained about you, which means there are others who haven't said anything. They all say you're heavy-handed." I didn't mention her personality issues.

In just seconds, her persona went from angry, to confused, to hurt. "Who complained?" she asked. "I don't believe this. I'm the only one here who really cares."

I stifled a comment. "Look. I can't say who. They obviously told me in confidence." Angry, I went for the throat. "Gums don't have to bleed profusely during a proper cleaning."

She snapped back, "Well, you're not a hygienist," as if I hadn't cleaned teeth for years when I first opened my practice.

I became more irritated. "Fran, you're not attuned to

people. You're obnoxious—with the patients, the staff, and with me. I actually dread coming to work on Tuesdays and Thursdays." Bam. She gasped in horror and began to shake. Tears flowed.

"You're gonna have to change the way you treat people," I said as I stood and left without even saying goodnight.

While I climbed the stairs to our kitchen, I heard Kate trying to reason with and comfort Fran. I went straight for the blender, firing it up to make strawberry daiquiris. The noise effectively drowned out Fran's crying.

Forty-five minutes later Kate stormed upstairs, glaring laser beams. I cowered. *Maybe I shouldn't have been so harsh.*

"Carroll. I don't believe the things you said to her."

"Me neither. It just came out."

She paused and nodded. "But they needed to be said."

Kate wasn't mad at me. She'd had it with Fran too and couldn't wait to gulp the daiquiri waiting for her. We soon loosened up enough to laugh about it.

A month later, while I recuperated from a hard day by lying on a heating pad, Kate came bounding into our bedroom, beaming.

"I have an early Christmas present for you. She's quitting."

Stunned, I sat up. "I don't think I heard you right."

"Fran gave notice. She found a job with more hours and benefits."

Kate said Fran was teary-eyed because she'd "never worked in such a friendly office." I guess she forgot about our little talk last month. Or she didn't care.

Kate sat on the edge of the bed. "It gets better. Tania called this afternoon. Her son's asthma is under control. She can start work in September when her boys go back to school. We'll just have to make do for a couple of weeks."

I'd never enjoyed prophys as much as during the last half of that August.

Despite having a chronically ill child, Tania had never missed a day of work during her first stint with us, except that one time when the big snowstorm blew through Gloyd and no one could dig out, except Tom the carpenter. *Farmer's Almanac* was now predicting a bad winter hard on the heels of November's first killing frost. TV weathermen projected a notable snowfall before Thanksgiving, which was early for Maryland. Although not a dire forecast, only a thirty percent chance, nervous suburbanites emptied grocery store shelves. *Is it really necessary to stock up on Oreos and Cokes?* I wondered.

"If it snows tonight, I don't think I'll be in tomorrow," Tania sheepishly announced on the way out that evening. "But I'll call early in the morning if I can't make it."

The following day dawned bright and sunny. Serous clouds streaking across a deep blue winter sky scattered crisp sunbeams. It was gorgeous outside. Better yet, Tania was sure to be in.

Out of breath, she blasted through the office door, apologizing for being later than usual. While she usually came in a few minutes after everyone else due to her kid's bus schedules, I didn't mind. She was always ready for her first patient.

"The kids stayed up late thinking they wouldn't have school today. Those sleepyheads couldn't get going," she said. "I had to practically shove them out the door. Sometimes it seems like their feet are nailed to the floor."

Not like their mom, I thought. Tania trotted quickly down the hallway like the *Star Wars* character, Jar Jar Binks.

During lunch, I asked, "So, Tania. You're from Pennsylvania. Why don't you drive in snow?"

She stopped chewing, covered her mouth, and muttered to the floor, "I'm sorry."

"That's okay." I felt bad. "Just curious."

"I ... I once hit a deer." She stared down at her feet. "But not today. The kids made me late this morning." She looked up. "Actually ... it's been three deer ... three different times. All in bad weather, except once." Her eyes shifted but never looked directly at mine.

"Don't bother explaining, Tania. He's an idiot for asking," someone said. The other ladies around the lunch table agreed, as attested by the eyes that seared holes in me.

I tried to redeem myself. "Most folks around here have hit a deer or two. I have. It's no big deal." Tania forced a smile.

My mind drifted back to when our daughter Tara turned sixteen. She'd just gotten her driver's license when she ran into a deer on a sunny summer afternoon. It happened just over the bridge, on the other side of the Gloyd reservoir. Totally flustered after hitting it, Tara slammed on the brakes—a little too late to save the deer, which was already down. A few good ole boys fishing in the lake saw what happened and yelled up to her, "Ya need to just keep on moving, little gal."

All she heard was, "Back your car up." So that's what she did, running over the twitching doe a second time.

Tara returned home, crying all the while about the poor innocent animal she'd just murdered twice over. Yours truly spent Saturday afternoon cleaning fur and guts from her car's undercarriage. I thought I might lighten the mood by telling my staff about it.

Grinning with embarrassment, Tania said, "Yeah, but I totaled the car—all three times."

The staff turned as one to stare at her. "Three different cars," she added for emphasis. At least the ladies weren't glaring at me anymore.

"Wow. Bad luck, I guess," I said.

Every time Tania hit a deer, it retaliated by destroying her family van. Maybe it was time for her to invest in a Hummer, or an Abrams tank. For some stupid reason I pressed the issue. "But accidents with deer have little or nothing to do with snow."

She shrugged and went on to share her weather- and coffee-related accidents she'd had.

Before they'd cleared the table, the staff were howling about their own driving mishaps, each exploit outdoing the previous one. Misery does love company. I listened as unobtrusively as I could until they switched from crushed vehicles to hair salons and fingernails. I wondered how they could jump so quickly from one subject to another.

When the afternoon patients arrived early, I bounded down the office stairs, taking them two at a time to avoid any more small talk, especially about cars.

Note: No deer were run over during the composition of this story.

CHAPTER FIVE

Mexico and the Moth

F loating through a clear sky, I gazed out the window at a soft carpet of clouds below the Boeing 737. A couple of months earlier, a mailer had landed on my desk:

Tired of the same old grind?
Call: *Missionary Dentists.*

I was curious and dialed the number during my lunch hour.

"Good morning. Can I help you?" a pleasant lady answered.

Morning? "I'd like to ... err ... where are you located, and what do you do?"

"Seattle. We arrange for dentists to do volunteer work in impoverished countries. Are you a dentist?"

"Uh-huh." *Not very articulate, Carroll.*

"Have you ever been abroad on a short-term mission?"

"The Soviet Union in 1988." I hesitated before adding, "But that wasn't dental."

She suggested that Mexico would be a good first-time clinical experience. "It's an easy jaunt from the States."

First-time? "Uh ... okay."

Two months later, I was stuffing my clothes into a suitcase when our phone rang. "Carroll! It's for you," Kate called from the kitchen before joining me in the bedroom. "Let me help you." Exasperated with my packing, she pulled everything out and started folding.

"They're still waiting for you to pick up," she said.

"Will you accept the call?" an overseas operator asked.

"I guess?"

"Hi. Dr. James?" asked a crackly voice over the poor connection.

"Yes, I'm Carroll James."

"I'm Bob from Oaxaca, but you can just call me Bob!" *Funny guy.* "Can you ride a horse?"

"Yep, grew up on horseback."

"Great! I need a dentist who can ride because walking to the remote village I have in mind would take several days." His idea was to treat hard-to-reach folks in the rugged mountains along the Isthmus of Tehuantepec. "You can say good-bye to the twentieth century," Bob emphasized while laughing.

So much for an "easy jaunt," but it appealed to me because I would be helping folks like my Nealy Ridge forebears of southwestern Virginia. Despite a difference of language, appearance, and traditions, they're all basically hillbillies.

"Well, I guess I'm your man."

Travel guru, Rick Steves, preaches three basic rules: pack light, pack light, and ... pack light. It's something I had yet to learn. Bob said, "All ya need is pliers to pull teeth. About all we can do is get 'em out of pain." He laughed. He always laughed. "See ya in Veracruz."

Veracruz was a beautiful colonial port on the Gulf of Mexico. Tall ships, overburdened with Aztec gold, once sailed from there to brave the treacherous North Atlantic crossing. They sometimes made it to the Old Country but often didn't. Enter modern-day treasure hunters.

"How will I find you in the airport?" I shouted as Bob was about to hang up.

"I always wear a red baseball cap. Some nights the wife has to remind me to take it off." Seemed a bit sketchy. *But how many white guys with a red cap can there be in Veracruz?*

Mexico City was founded in a high mountain bowl surrounded by wind-swept peaks. Buffeted by the unpredictable currents, the Boeing 737 careened erratically on the long final approach. I was sweating bullets when we finally landed—hard.

Benito Juarez Terminal seemed small for a city of twenty-five million souls. Although unable to speak the language to ask for directions, I eventually stumbled across the luggage carousel. It groaned under the weight of bags overloaded by Mexicans returning home with myriad goods: TVs, microwaves, VCRS, small refrigerators, etc. I even saw the proverbial kitchen sink.

In contrast, my Samsonite bulged with shorts, T-shirts, extra shoes, rain gear, a couple of hats, several cans of bug spray, and enough SPF 30 to protect the entire Swedish sunbathing team. Dental supplies were crammed into my navy duffle along with extra underwear.

In the heat, a dense throng of sweaty folks funneled toward a series of traffic lights. Dragging my heavy bag, I asked a uniformed officer what to do, but he just angrily gestured, so I watched the locals while I inched forward.

A large button that resembled a flat doorknob separated the red and green lights. Folks hit it with their palm, the green light flashed, and they sashayed through with their bags. *Easy enough.* When I finally got to the front, I whacked the knob, and walked on.

"*Señor ... señor! Alto.*" I didn't see who called out to me, but the red light was lit. A guard grabbed my arm and escorted me to a chipped Formica table that rocked on uneven legs. He pointed to my luggage. "*Abrir.*"

"What?"

"Open theem, pleeze."

He grinned at the socks and Jockeys Kate had neatly folded, but then he became deadly serious when he saw latex gloves, needles, and syringes in my duffle. He frantically riffled through it and discovered boxes of Lidocaine carpules. He stared long and hard at me. I didn't think I could sweat any more in this heat. I was wrong. *I thought all Mexicans were short.* Not this one.

"What es these, *señor?* Drugs?"

My mind whirled. I felt dizzy. *He thinks I'm smuggling.* "I'm a dentist. That's local anesthetic." I grinned a silly smile. "I'm pretty sure no one smuggles drugs *into* this country."

He sneered and pulled out a walkie-talkie. Another customs agent stormed over and ordered my bags dumped onto the table. "Empty pockets," he said. He inspected my ADA license and made a phone call—a long one. For some reason, he allowed me to pass, with my drugs. After several trips, I decided that the lights were calibrated to gringo sweat; I always got stopped.

In the meantime, my layover time had dwindled to almost nothing. A pleasant lady noticed me frantically searching the terminal. She came over and looked at my ticket, smiled, and pointed the way to my gate. I must've looked like a lost puppy.

"*Gracias.*" About all the Spanish I knew.

"Have a nice flight." Her English was perfect.

I've got to learn the language.

After waiting in another security line for the short hop to Veracruz, I strolled confidently through the metal detector. The attendant grabbed me and pulled me over to yet another wobbly table. This wasn't going well. He was upset about the small pocketknife I'd nonchalantly placed into the coin basket (this was pre-911).

My Uncle Joel gave me that knife when I was a kid; it was a treasured possession. Tired and frustrated, I wasn't about to give it up without a fight.

"It's just a tool, for crying out loud," I protested. I don't think he understood a word, but for another unknown reason, he waved me through. I'd have been thrown into jail today. As it was, I barely made the flight.

The aircraft's cabin was worse than ratty. Though I knew it didn't need to be pretty to fly, my seat wouldn't click into the upright position. The flight attendant, who probably saw the altercation over the penknife, might've thought I was still being uncooperative. "*Señor*, put seat up for takeoff."

"I can't. It has a mind of its own."

"No mind. Straight up, *por favor*."

I've since learned to avoid colloquialisms. "Look, it won't latch."

"You broke?" She leaned in.

"No. Already broke." Pigeon English didn't work any better.

"Back up, if pleeze."

"Okay … whatever." I reached over my head and yanked it upright, holding it while she turned to berate other passengers. Takeoff was bumpy, and I totally lost my grip on the seat as we climbed steeply to clear the mountains. I ended up reclining on the guy's knees behind me. *This must be where old Boeing 727s go to die.*

Touchdown in Veracruz was again hard; the brakes screeched, then locked, propelling my seat upright. The attendant was happy. So was the guy behind me.

Back on terra firma, I started to breathe easy until the aging craft shuddered and turned one-eighty to taxi back along the landing strip. A rusty staircase slammed against the fuselage, and the cabin door opened to an oppressive heat. My shirt quickly became drenched in sweat while I trekked across the gooey tarmac toward a warehouse-looking box. I prayed for air-conditioning, but that wasn't gonna happen.

The heat was more oppressive inside where the air was

heavy with stench. Black fans sporting frayed electric cords, and without blade guards, sat on various countertops. They oscillated erratically in a futile attempt to attack the stale heat.

I scanned the small airport for a Yanqui in a red hat; none was in sight. I also couldn't find baggage claim or any conveyer belt that carried luggage in an endless circle. Frustrated, I asked for help. "Where suitcases?" I again tried pigeon English. Bad move. The armed guard stared me down while fingering his holster. "Okay ... I'll just step outside. No problem-o, sir." I thought adding an 'o' might help. It didn't.

I stumbled outside and noticed passengers crowding around suitcases erratically lined up on the heat-softened, tar-soaked tarmac. My two bags had been offloaded while I wandered aimlessly through the terminal. I grabbed my suitcase and winced; the handle was scalding, yet I had to tug to free it from the goo. My canvas duffle had become one with the asphalt and almost refused to let go. I thought of the Tar Baby.

I carried my suitcase and dragged my sticky duffle, heavy with stainless steel instruments, back into the terminal, keeping my eyes peeled for a bright red hat. When I re-entered, the big guard glared at me. I gave him a wide berth while making several large circuits.

The number of travelers had dwindled when I noticed a portly, middle-aged fellow with a ruddy-Anglo mug and beige baseball cap who also seemed lost—two kindred souls circling aimlessly. Looking closely, I realized that his hat wasn't off-white, but rather a badly faded red. I've since learned that the American who doesn't wear that dumbstruck tourist expression is probably the missionary.

"You must be Carroll." Bob's broad, award-winning smile reflected an inner peace. He slapped me on the back. "Good to meet you. Wait here while I get my truck." He soon pulled up in a weather-beaten, four-wheel drive that matched his beat-up hat. A woman climbed out of the front seat. "This is my wife." Flo was his life-long helpmate in bringing aid to impoverished folks.

"It's nice to meet you." I shook her hand while Bob threw my luggage into the back. "Be careful, Bob. There's a lot of gunk on the bottom of those bags."

"That's okay. It happens." The Suburban's cargo floor had accumulated enough tar to seal my driveway. Graciously, Flo climbed into the back seat so I could sit up front.

The "highway" to Tuxtepec was a one-and-a-half lane deathtrap that presented my first look at the pervasive poverty. Some of the flimsy stick-shacks had tin roofs, but most were thatch. The walls would only discourage a good rain, forget about a Caribbean hurricane.

A constant parade of ragged peasants, many barefoot, shuffled along the dusty shoulder, overloaded with baskets of produce, bundles of firewood, pails of brown water, bulging burlap sacks, and other packs. One *campesino* suddenly cut across, directly in front of us. Riding shotgun, I hit my non-existent brake and nearly put my foot through the rusted floorboard. Bob honked, swerved, and smiled. It was second nature to him. The jaywalker never looked up.

Horses, burros, and mules were almost as numerous as people. The livestock trudged along with burdens seemingly larger than themselves. Other animals were staked to graze in the ditch where the grass was nominally green. Some wandered loose, crossing whenever their fancy struck, just like the people. Chickens strutted about—except for the dead ones that had been run over.

As we careened hell-bent down Highway 145, a glorified moniker for a potholed ribbon of death, Bob sped up to pass an overloaded produce truck. I averted my eyes and braced for impact with an oncoming car, but curiosity got the better of me and I squinted through my fingers. The oncoming car moved over at the last possible moment, which created three lanes out of two. We were in the middle one, flanked by the tottering truck and dented car.

Shortly afterward, Bob swerved toward the shoulder when an oncoming vehicle passed an ox wagon. As we veered wildly, pedestrians and livestock sidestepped into the drainage ditch without looking up. They seemed to have a sixth sense about it that made it all surreal.

This wasn't a game of chicken, but rather a carefully choreographed traffic pattern. It was never clear, at least to me, which vehicle should give way, but the drivers always seemed to know. Besides, it was the only way to get past those slow trucks spewing black smoke and mule-drawn carts that left piles of manure on the road. Flo, smiling all the while, was comfortably ensconced in the back while I sweated bullets. *Wish Bob hadn't insisted that I sit up front.*

While we headed south, the sun slowly set, enveloping the countryside in darkness. There were no streetlights; many vehicles lacked headlights and few had taillights. The thrill of Latino-style travel was kicked up a notch in the pitch black of night.

Oaxaca was Mexico's most destitute state and Tuxtepec its poorest city. A decrepit billboard, framed by dim forty-watt bulbs, half of which were out, proclaimed a city of 50,000 souls. Under layers of ancient grime, another sign at the southwestern approach boasted 300,000. Probably somewhere in between?

Bob suddenly hung a sharp right and bounced violently through the dry drainage ditch. With no seat belts, my head slammed against the ceiling. We screeched to a halt in a cloud of choking dust. Unlike the muffler, the brakes worked quite well. Bob heartily laughed and announced, "Time for dinner."

I was a little stiff climbing out, but my tailbone was thankful to be off that coiled spring poking through the cracked vinyl seat. It was like escaping a hot steel tomb festooned with spikes. *Maybe I'll donate new shock absorbers to the cause.*

The open-air restaurant was little more than a glorified food stand. I gingerly sat on a rickety plastic chair at a dirty-white plastic table. Salsa music blared from two bullhorn speakers that hung precariously from a crumbling cement wall surrounding the dirt courtyard. The proprietor emerged from a small blockhouse that housed the kitchen.

"Bob and Flo—*mi amigos!*"

They introduced me and, before I knew what was happening, I was getting a bear hug. The plastic chair ominously groaned under the pressure. In this non-tourist region, folks went out of their way to make me feel at home. Their warm, friendly smiles were genuine and not of the purchased variety.

The owner snapped his fingers and a groveling waiter dressed in a filthy apron over baggy pants, a sleeveless T-shirt, and flip flops, handed out greasy menus. After they retired to the kitchen with our dinner order, Bob and Flo recited inviolable dining rules. Over the garish music turned up to the max, I heard every fourth word—maybe.

"Anything you order is fine," I shouted. "Can't read the menu anyway," although *taco, burrito,* and *enchilada* were familiar. They spoke louder, which helped. Having been married for an eternity, they always finished each other's sentences:

"Vegetables are irrigated with *brown water* ..."

"... which is to say sewage."

"Fresh produce may look inviting but is often unfit."

"If peeled tableside, it's okay ..."

"... but only eat the protected layers inside."

"Always order a bottled drink and never pour it into a glass ..."

"... that's likely been washed in tainted tap water."

"Drink straight from the bottle, but first wipe it off with your shirttail ..."

"... which is probably cleaner, regardless of how long you've worn it."

The list goes on, but while I learned most of my safe eating tips that night, GI distress in the mission field has been an ongoing fight—replacement salts and Imodium have been invaluable.

Although I was famished, it seemed like we waited an eternity for our food. Like everything else, restaurants operated on *Latino time*. It'll be ready, when it's ready, regardless of when you were told it would be ready, and no sooner—or later. So sit back, relax, and enjoy the music ... *la cucaracha, la cucaracha* ....

With fork in hand, I was perched for the kill when our piping hot chow finally appeared, but I paused when Bob and Flo bowed their heads. With missionaries, grace can be a mini-sermon. Thankfully, this one was short. When Bob finished, he pointed at the lettuce. "Probably washed in *brown* water." Yuk.

"Anything cooked is okay," Flo reiterated. The meal was tasty, or maybe I was just hungry. The meat was hard to identify, but I suspected some kind of fowl.

Floodlights propped atop two corner poles of the dusty patio were much brighter than the town's billboard. They attracted myriad bugs in the hot, humid stillness of the jungle evening. Many were quite large and distinctly ugly. Working in cahoots, I imagined they could probably lift the meat off our plates.

One particularly persistent varmint kept buzzing my right ear. Not wanting to make a scene, I nonchalantly swept him aside, but time and again he returned, maybe because I didn't put up a determined defense (I didn't want to appear wimpy by flailing). He dive-bombed the same ear—always the right one, never the left. *Maybe I spilled food on my collar.*

Bent low over their own plates, Bob and Flo didn't notice my battle with the mammoth moth. *Now's my chance.* I snapped my head to the right to confront my tormentor, but instead of a large moth, a huge lizard with a nasty jagged spine was perched on my shoulder. Its right *hand* held my collar while its left one tormented my ear.

Taken by surprise, I spun to the left and nearly fell off my wobbly chair. Startled, the brazen pest scurried down my arm and jumped onto my dinner plate. After pausing to inspect my food, he performed a *salsa* victory dance on the rice, meat, and vegetables. The lettuce was no longer the only thing that was unappetizing.

Flo glanced up while the intruder moonwalked across my food, then leaned over to casually flick him off like a bothersome fly at a picnic. Indignant at such rude treatment, the reptile scampered away.

I smiled nervously and tried to regain my cool in front of people I'd just met, then thought about the lizard-infested jungle I was headed for tomorrow. Ten days of adventure remained. Surely I could tough it out. After all, I'd been exposed to various vermin in southwestern Virginia when I was a kid, but the reptiles on The Ridge weren't Godzilla-size.

CHAPTER SIX

Still Hot

After that prehistoric lizard scurried off my plate, I managed to choke down some dinner—leaving out the lettuce. In the middle of Tuxtepec, Bob drove through an iron gate and entered a courtyard defined by an eight-foot wall and three conjoined concrete buildings. In the center, a towering palm tree was ringed by decorative stones and a flowerbed in full bloom. Neatly trimmed shrubs bordered the walkways, and a carefully weeded vegetable garden sat proudly behind a communal kitchen. Flower pots on the second-floor roof alternated with vertical rebar that anticipated a third story.

The compound housed a school sanctuary for about thirty young women rescued from a degrading life on the streets. Their rooms were located on the first floor, while the staff occupied apartments off a second-floor catwalk. A peaceful oasis in which to learn and work, it had the feel of an extended family.

Bob was the maintenance man. Flo taught music. Their flat was comprised of a small living room, eat-in kitchen, tiny bedroom, and a guest room. "You're in here, *amigo*." Bob laughed as he pushed a door that creaked open to an overheated room with four bunk beds for visiting medical teams. It reeked of stale body odor worse than a boy's locker room. Sometimes more than eight people were crammed inside when a large aid group passed through.

Flo pulled a chain and the one ceiling fan hesitantly moved the heavy air. As the only guest, I had my choice of bunks, each with a threadbare mattress on thin plywood.

"I like the one under the fan," I announced.

After placing my toiletries on a tottering wooden stand beside my bunk, I wandered into the kitchenette where Flo had a pot of water boiling on the stove. "Can't send you boys off without drinking water."

I nodded and affected a quick retreat to the living room. "You know, Bob, it's nice in here—almost cool."

"*Cool* is relative." He picked up a battered thermometer. "It's a *mere* ninety-seven degrees Fahrenheit in here," Bob said with a chuckle. The flip side of the gauge read thirty-six degrees Celsius, which sounded better. I didn't ask how hot it was in the kitchen—I didn't want to know.

I spent the night tossing in a puddle of sweat while the sounds of restless animals disturbed the humid air: donkeys brayed, sheep baaed, pigs grunted, and roosters crowed with no sense of timing, apparently confused by the city lights. I might've been on a farm except the ruckus included blaring horns and sultry music blasted from dozens of nightclubs and hundreds, thousands, of radios. The squeal of car brakes was often followed by a sickening thud; another wandering chicken had met his Maker. The deafening cacophony, along with Bob's constant snoring, didn't play well with my insomnia.

The fan's palm frond blades projected slowly turning shadows on the crumbling plaster walls and sparse furnishings. Despite the fan's best efforts, I freely perspired and began to chortle like a crazy person. Mesmerized by its wobble, my eyes finally closed with a weighty weariness.

Suddenly, my lids fluttered open when I heard heavenly music drifting through the open window. *Maybe I died and angels have come for me?* The young girls were singing while going about their early morning chores of laundry, cleaning, and cooking. Although sung in Spanish, I recognized many of the songs. Music was a universal language.

I lollygagged on my damp bedroll in a futile attempt to steal a few more winks, but the aroma of fresh-brewed coffee beckoned. Lard sizzled. *Do I smell hash browns?* Bacon crackled in an iron skillet. Eggs were cracked and scrambled. My mouth watered, remembering Grandma's fresh-baked pocketbook bread. I surrendered and rubbed the sleep from my eyes before stumbling down to the dining hall.

But breakfast wasn't at all like Grandma's. The runny eggs were mixed with hot peppers, chopped onions, diced tomatoes, and gallons of fire-breathing salsa. The rocket-fuel coffee was palatable when thinned with a generous helping of goat's milk. There was no bacon, no fried potatoes, and no freshly baked bread—I'd only imagined them.

Nevertheless, I dug in while Bob loaded meager supplies into his road-weary SUV for our journey to a remote village. Already running late, I downed a last bite and threw my instrument duffle onto the asphalt-sticky truck floor. After I hopped in, the girls smiled and waved good-bye. Bob floored it and entered the heavy traffic with reckless abandon. *So yesterday's death-drive wasn't just a bad dream.*

Bouncing along on the tired shocks, we left town and crossed the isthmus before turning south toward the foreboding mountains hard at the Guatemalan border. "Zapatista rebels control this area, but they won't bother us," Bob nonchalantly announced.

"I'm sure you're right," I echoed, but I wasn't sure.

A sad stretch of road with more potholes than pavement crossed a mountain pass. Bob slowed as a roadblock came into view. A group of young insurgents were crowded around a rusty pickup truck they'd stopped with a sturdy chain strung between two trees, which could be raised and lowered by a hand-winch manned by two toothless old men.

A shirtless young rebel shoved a rusted coffee can through the truck's window. The toll booth would've been comical if not for his AK47-wielding comrade, reminding me of the disciplined young guards in Moscow, except these guys didn't look trained.

The truck paid the toll and moved on. Bob pulled up, then said, "I'm not giving these buggers money." He punched the accelerator and we lurched forward, careening over the chain that now lay on the dirt. Blood drained from my face. "Riding shotgun" took on new meaning as I dove for the floor. "I'll donate a few pesos!" I shouted from below.

I half expected warning shots but only heard the rattling roar of our old engine. Hesitant, I sat up and looked for a pursuit car. Through the dust kicked up by our bald tires, I saw the group of insurgents still milling about, seemingly unfazed by our arrogance.

Bob grinned and threw his head back in a hearty laugh, his cheeks far rosier than his faded cap. His ample belly shook, but when he noticed how shocked I looked, he said, "They always block that pass—done so for years. Government doesn't care." He'd paid the toll several times but soon tired of the extortion. The pitiful beggars knew him; they were aware that he was helping their people and didn't have much money himself. I wished I'd known that before slamming my head against the glove box on my way to the floor.

(This particular tribe of Native Americans was highlighted in the news a few years later. They'd actively rebelled against the government with loss of life on both sides. As is common with such venting, the locals suffered most.)

Shortly after leaving the desperadoes behind, we turned

onto a dilapidated stretch of the Pan American Highway. Cruising along with the bright sunshine and wind in my face, I was glad to be alive. The magnificent Sierra Madre del Sur loomed in the near distance as we turned onto a side road. With huge craters for potholes, it was impassable during the rainy season. "Been stuck here in axle-deep mud," Bob said. "Dust is better."

For several hours, we dodged huge boulders, deep chasms, stray cows, angry bulls, half-starved chickens, stubborn burros, emaciated dogs, and a rooting pig. We finally arrived at an ancient highland village that boasted but one claim to fame: they had never surrendered to the *conquistadores*.

These Chinentacos conversed in their native tongue. Men who worked in the fertile valleys for absentee landowners spoke Spanish, but the women seldom did. Spanish was as foreign to the kids as Klingon.

Their clothing was ragged—men wore slacks, seldom jeans, boots or tennis shoes, and cotton shirts. Hats varied: straw, cowboy, baseball, and even fedoras. I never saw one *sombrero*.

Women were rarely dressed in anything modern, but rather wore brightly colored, homespun skirts and blouses and heavy traditional wraps. Many ladies wore head scarves to shield themselves from the intense sun. Umbrellas were prevalent—not sure where they got them.

Children weren't adequately clothed, and none had shoes with the exception of one young lad, who strutted proudly in his cowboy boots. He didn't have pants or underwear, and his cotton shirt hung open, but he seemed happy. His broad smile spoke volumes.

Everyday life was similar to that of their distant ancestors. Smoke from cooking fires drifted through the hot, humid air. Intermittent electrical power served a few light bulbs hanging from frayed wires where a toaster would've blown the town's circuit. Bob's was the only car in the village. Modern conveniences were few. Plumbing was nonexistent.

In the faint glow of early dawn and in the purple haze of a setting sun, women plied rocky paths to fetch water from a stream a half hour down the mountain. They carried it in decorative clay jugs balanced atop their heads, keeping a pace that would've been hard for me to match without a heavy load. I witnessed only one man carrying water, with two metal buckets hanging from a pole balanced on the nape of his neck. He smiled for a picture, unfazed by performing "women's work." He was a member of the small church that hosted our dental mission.

Fowl was a common denominator for meals. After wringing the chicken necks, the women scalded them before plucking their feathers. After adding various roots, herbs, and vegetables, they used the same boiled water to cook with. Pork or beef was served only on special occasions—and we weren't that special. Chicken it would be for the next ten days.

A church elder offered his humble hut for Bob and me to call home. It consisted of walls of rough-hewn planks bound together with hemp that supported a thatched roof. There were no windows, only sizable gaps through which some daylight filtered.

A colorful blanket draped over a rope separated the parents' chamber from that of their kids. They graciously relinquished their bedroom so I could sleep in private. Bob slept on a coarse blanket spread on the dirt floor in the common room with everyone else. Humbled, I tried to think of the last time I gave up my bed to a total stranger. *Never.*

Furnishings were sparse, and a few wooden pegs on the walls sufficed as hangers. The bed was burlap stuffed with straw. Next to it, a wire corncrib attracted all sorts of vermin that plagued me throughout the night and were periodically picked off by ravenous lizards that scurried across me. While tossing and turning, I kept one arm draped over my eyes to protect them.

It was hot with no breeze coming through the cracks. Itching all over, I coveted the slowly turning shadows projected by that old ceiling fan in the Tuxtepec bunkhouse.

I arose before dawn to the call of nature and groped through the dark, stumbling over the sleeping bodies of the family. Bob stirred but didn't awaken. Tiptoeing outside, I stretched and deeply inhaled the morning air, finding it refreshing.

When we arrived the previous evening, I'd noticed an outhouse "for such a time as this." What I'd failed to see in the dim twilight was that it not only lacked a door, but it faced the main trail. I hesitated, but yesterday's loose eggs got to me. It was quite early and no one was around.

I stepped inside and tripped over a wooden bucket, spilling corncobs across the ground. Panicky, I remembered that Ole Mister Chadwick stocked corncobs in his Nealy Ridge privy. Then I searched for anything that resembled toilet paper. I'd noticed a roll stashed in Bob's glove box but hadn't thought anything of it, until now.

I ran back and found the truck locked. Bob was still asleep. I desperately paced, waiting for him to rise with sun. Going back inside the hut, I *accidentally* tripped over him. "Sorry, Bob."

"That's okay, *compadre*." He leaned up on one elbow and wiped the sleep from his eyes. "You're up early."

"Couldn't sleep. Do you have the truck keys?"

I grabbed the ring and ran to fetch the roll, probably the only one in town. I barely made it and sat on the wooden hole, relieved.

In the meantime, the village awoke. The women trekked past my open doorway and gave me a friendly smile before heading down the mountain with their empty water jugs. A few kids came by, lingered, pointed, and giggled before running away. I smiled and gave them a little wave. There was no room for modesty in the mission field.

Breakfast was granola bars, trail mix, and coffee. Not wanting to reload, I didn't eat.

Of all the medical teams he had worked with, Bob especially liked dentists. The instruments to extract a tooth are minimal and the work relieves folks of their pain. It could be lifesaving if the infection was severe. He knew how to make do, so I followed his lead as he established our clinic in the village square. He had the Indians place a door-sized plank on two sawhorse-looking things. I wished they'd first used it as an outhouse door.

On this makeshift counter, I arranged my instruments. The silver gleamed in the morning sun as the natives gawked. I also laid out anesthetics, gloves, gauze, and two plastic pans that Bob had scrounged up—one for rinse water and the other for my sterilizing solution. At my feet, a wooden bucket doubled as a trashcan and cuspidor. I learned to say spit, *escupir*, while pointing at it and away from me. Unfortunately, I often overthrew the bucket when tossing extracted teeth toward it, and dogs hovered close to fight over remnants that bounced onto the ground. I was never any good at basketball.

Patients sat in a simple wooden chair. With few exceptions, they were all short and I had to stoop low, which put a strain on my back until I figured out that cinder bricks or paint cans—or even large rocks if nothing else was available— would bring them up to my height. My "dental chair" was periodically rotated as the sun, which was my mouth light, coursed through the sky. The workday was over at sundown or when it rained.

One of the village elders sacrificially offered his young daughter as my first patient. *Best to test the gringo's skill.* I smiled as she squirmed. "So what seems to be the problem?"

Bob rendered my question into Spanish, which was then

translated by an elder into Chinentaco. The poor girl looked like she wanted to run away. The translator explained her problem in Spanish, and Bob related it in English. Each diagnosis—question and answer—took this long, circuitous route.

After we finally agreed which tooth to pull—she actually needed several out, but I only did what they wanted done—I injected the local anesthetic. Her wide-eyed peers grimaced, but the cute kid sat stoically motionless. After waiting for the numbing juice to work its magic, I instructed, "Open wide and stay real still." After a brief interlude for interpretation, she closed her eyes and obediently opened. Immediately, a fly flew into and out of her gaping maw. The crowd got a good laugh while she squeezed her eyes tighter, not knowing what had happened.

She remained stock-still as I applied pressure to the tooth, which easily came out. "All finished. Bite on this gauze and change it every half hour." She stood and smiled that familiar crooked Novocaine grin. At this point, language differences didn't matter; I could see that she was genuinely grateful. Thrilled to be pain-free, she trumpeted my skill throughout the village. Folks clambered to get in line.

Determining which tooth to extract could be a challenge. "Only take the painful ones out, Dr. C," Bob said.

"But they'll start bothering them after I leave," I countered, wanting to do it right.

"Doesn't matter. Only do what they want. Just get 'em out of pain." Bob explained that we were walking a fine line, not only with the local authorities, but also with the central government.

After ten hours of back-breaking work, I was spent. My aching body welcomed the dying radiance of the sun as it set behind the western peaks. Despite some post-operative discomfort, my patients were all smiles, patting my back as I wearily shuffled home.

That night an elderly parishioner invited us to dinner. Maybe it was exhaustion, but boiled chicken never tasted so good. After thanking him and his wife, we headed down a dark lane to our adopted hovel. That night was as hot and sticky as before, with just as many roaming vermin, but I slept like a log and didn't awaken until the cocks crowed at dawn.

A young couple invited us to their hut for a scrumptious breakfast—brown eggs scrambled with hot peppers over a piping-hot tortilla energized me for another hard but rewarding day.

Later that morning, a crowd was gathered in the square, rubbing painful jaws. Self-appointed assistants had already set up the clinic and begun to screen them. Things were running smoothly when, after only a few patients, Bob announced that he had to leave. Nervously, I asked, "So when do you think you'll be back?"

"Don't know. Later today."

My gut felt hollow. "So who's gonna interpret?"

"You'll be fine, Doc. You've already got the hang of it and they know what's going on now. Just point and gesture." He laughed and turned to leave with an Indian who came to fetch him. While walking away, they started singing. The tune faded as they disappeared down a dark trail, swallowed by the jungle.

Me? A little unnerved, I didn't feel like singing. So far these folks had been friendly, but what if something went wrong?

Despite my trepidation, work went smoothly for the next couple hours until a powerful young buck stepped forward. Unsmiling, he plopped onto the tottering chair and warily eyed me as I picked up a probe. He winced when I touched the offending tooth, then flexed his muscular forearms. *Maybe as a warning?*

I began to sweat bullets. *What happened to all those small villagers?* After numbing him, I tugged and the tooth broke, its roots firmly embedded in his jaw. I continued to wrestle with them but saw little hope that I'd get them out. Perspiration beaded across my forehead.

My muscles strained for one final attempt when the chair suddenly moved and threatened to fall off the cinder blocks. But I held on, my arm nearly wrenched from its socket. The root pulled free. The bloody stump dangled from my hand.

The Indians who crowded around, fascinated by the struggle, now howled with laughter. Even my patient broke into a cockeyed smile, blood trickling from the corner of his mouth. Grinning sheepishly, I patted his back while gesturing for the next person in line.

Bob returned shortly thereafter. "Hey, Dr. C. Did you feel that earth tremor?" he asked. "It was a doozy. I'll check the news when we get back to Tuxtepec, but that might've been a full-blown earthquake." The colliding of tectonic plates, of which I had been clueless, had possibly jolted the tooth free.

Although I got pretty good at pitching bloody teeth into the pail, I knew I'd overshot when the sad, emaciated dogs began to fight over it. Curiously, the dogs never bothered the chickens pecking around my feet. The only healthy ones in town were well-fed hunters, kept kenneled or tied up.

Dogs and chickens weren't the only distractions—children jostled for position to watch me work. Due to the heat I wore shorts, and on a dare, a kid might sneak up and touch my pale legs before affecting an innocent air by looking at the sky or whistling.

Except for my balding head, I wasn't smooth-skinned like the other men. One brazen lad plucked a strand from my thigh and darted away through a forest of brown legs, holding his trophy high while his buddies giggled. Another kid followed suit. It hurt and distracted me from work, but after a while I managed to ignore them.

After several days, it was time to leave. The broad smiles and lingering hugs of my new friends didn't make parting easy. They crowded so close to the Suburban that I had a hard time climbing in. When Bob fired it up, they reluctantly receded. I shut the door, looked out my open window, and saw a phalanx of hands waving amidst the cloud of dust we'd kicked up. I smiled and weakly waved back.

I wondered, *When I get back home, how will I explain to my dental friends the joy in such brutally hard work?*

I've never been able to.

After a short R&R at the mission house, Bob planned to take me into a remote region. I looked forward to it, but anxiously wondered if those primitives would be friendly, fierce, or a little of both. I slept little in the hot bunkhouse that night, thinking about our journey into those foreboding mountains.

CHAPTER SEVEN

Usila

The following morning, I climbed sleepy-eyed into Bob's truck for a short ride to an airstrip on the outskirts of town. While bouncing along a rutted dirt road, a sickening thud jolted me awake. I looked back and saw feathers everywhere. "Bob, I think we just hit a chicken."

"It happens." He slammed on his brakes, too late for the hen, then turned sharply into a narrow tree-lined lane and skidded to a stop at a terminal—a simple thatched roof supported by four rough-hewn wooden poles. It shaded a patch of dirt where grass all but refused to grow and was devoid of chairs or benches.

A couple of sad-looking huts were out by the grass strip. A rusted table, with a metal office chair chained to it, was bolted to one. It was shaded by a torn beach umbrella.

"I wonder where the clerk is," Bob mused. The only fellow in sight stood on a stepladder, bending over the engine of an antique Piper Cub, the only airplane around. A sweaty T-shirt rode up his backside while his ill-fitting slacks traveled south. Bob sauntered over to chat with him.

"That's our ride," he sullenly announced. He told Flo that we would be okay and she could leave. "We'll head over the mountains as soon as it's fixed." Flo kissed him and floored the Suburban, enveloping us in a cloud of dust.

I walked over to the plane to check out the open toolbox on the ground, which contained a couple of ball-peen hammers, a few ratty screwdrivers, several rusty wrenches, and sundry spark plugs. The mechanic was whacking the engine with a pipe wrench.

Bob sought shade under the terminal's thatch. Already drenched in sweat at eight o'clock in the morning, I joined him. "How long do you figure?" I asked, hopeful.

"Not long," which meant nothing in Mexico. He plopped onto the dirt/grass and I followed suit. While the guy banged on the Cub, I had a horrible thought. *I hope he's not the pilot.* But I was afraid to ask.

Over the next four hours, the temperature climbed to one hundred and three degrees Fahrenheit in the shade. Breathing became an effort and I drank my canteen dry. To ignore the thirst I tried pacing, but the intense sun forced me back under the thatch.

Sometime after high noon, the mechanic pulled his head out of the engine compartment, shuffled across the field, and disappeared into one of the shacks.

"Do you think he's finished?" I asked.

"Nah. *Siesta.*" Bob didn't even look up.

Antsy, I walked over and looked inside the plane. There was only one seat—for the pilot. "Hey, Bob. Where do we sit?"

He laughed. "On the floor. We're just cargo, *amigo.*"

"Uh, okay. When do you think we might leave?"

"Dunno." He lay on his back, folded his beefy hands over his rotund belly, and pulled the faded baseball cap over his eyes. I eyeballed the parched ground, shrugged my shoulders, and joined him.

While staring up at the myriad bugs swarming through the thatch, I heard what sounded like a flight of bees. A small plane buzzed the field, circled, and landed in a huge dust storm. I realized I hadn't seen or heard another aircraft all day: no jets, props, helicopters, blimps, kites, or paper airplanes. Other than birds, it was the only thing that flew.

"Why did it buzz the strip before landing?" I asked Bob.

"To clear it of stray animals or kids," he said, implying it was commonplace.

A young man sporting mirrored sunglasses climbed out and strutted confidently across the field. He wore a collared shirt, trim jeans, and polished cowboy boots. Bob quickly struggled to his feet and struck up negotiations with him. I prayed the pilot would take us over the mountains in his obviously airworthy plane. Bob turned and grinned, giving me two thumbs up.

"All right!" I said.

The maintenance man returned from his *siesta* and joined their discussion. He retrieved his monkey wrench and removed three of the four seats. So much for having a place to sit.

At that point, another unshaven, un-showered *hombre* emerged from one of the sheds and pulled back a canvas tarp that covered several cases of beer and unmarked boxes. The two grunts crammed it all inside the plane before stuffing in our meager supplies. My dental instruments came last. "Be careful," I pleaded to no avail, as my duffle was tossed like a gunny sack.

Bob squeezed into a tight niche by the far window. Houdini couldn't have curled up tighter. He leaned over and beckoned. "Hop in, Dr. Carroll."

I hesitated. "Sure. But where?" *And how will we take off with all this weight?*

He encouraged me by patting the top of a beer crate. I scrunched down, sucked in my gut, and climbed aboard. Bob noticed his projector box still on the ground.

"Can you hand me that, *amigo?*"

That's what I think he said—it was in Spanish—because the ground crew shoved it onto my lap. My head was wedged between it and the hot metal roof.

The temperature must've soared twenty degrees when the door was shut. I freely perspired while the pilot slowly climbed aboard. He propped his window open and buckled his seat belt, bantering with his friends while Bob and I baked in the metal tomb.

I closed my eyes to keep out the salty sweat and imagined cool air filtering through the cabin. It wasn't my imagination; we were, in fact, bouncing down the grass strip while my head slammed against the roof. Once airborne, the ride wasn't so bad despite the erratic updrafts streaming off the craggy mountains.

My starboard window afforded a magnificent view of the dark green jungle and a narrow valley divided by a glittering river. The blanket of lush foliage that crept up the mountainsides was occasionally split by the silver thread of a tributary.

When the valley widened, our macho pilot shoved his control stick forward, which again slammed my head against the roof and left my stomach in the clouds. We leveled off and skimmed the treetops a little too close for comfort until a clearing appeared. Then the plane further dropped to chase possible stray pigs, cows, chickens, or people off the landing strip. We banked steeply and came around to land; I was thankful when we finished taxiing. My head couldn't take any more abuse.

At the edge of the field, children clamored dangerously close to the still-whirling propeller. Bob briefly greeted them before scurrying down a narrow path that disappeared into the jungle. We were six hours behind schedule, late even by local standards. He went to find the porters and pack mules he'd reserved several weeks ago. "They should be waiting here," he said.

Bob had previously taken medical teams to a few outlying villages, and he'd recently heard of a remote one high in the mountains. That town's porters had waited, but they left in time to get home before dark. The jungle was dangerous at night when big cats were on the prowl.

For now, we were stuck here in Usila, a picturesque village huddled along a narrow strip of bottom land that lined a river of the same melodic name. Soaring mountain peaks framed the valley, east and west. Although we hadn't eaten a morsel since breakfast, I was too enamored of the place to notice my complaining stomach.

Volunteers brought our supplies from the plane to the mission house, which surprisingly was locked. Bob plopped onto a log, leaned his head on his hand, and weighed our options.

"Let's unroll our sleeping bags right here. It doesn't look like rain. Tomorrow, we'll set up shop in that clearing over there. We'll have plenty of work."

While I unpacked my bedroll and toiletries, an elderly gentleman stole quietly into the mission yard. "*Hola, señor.*" I nearly jumped out of my skin.

He and Bob spoke for a couple of minutes. "He's offering to feed us."

"I'm game."

"*Gracias.*" Bob smiled at him. The Indian's leathered visage returned a broad, partially toothless grin. Apparently another dentist had already made the rounds here.

The Good Samaritan led us along a darkening path toward his hut. Several children lined the trail to gawk at the white guys. His wife had made a stew that was unidentifiable in the dim candlelight but tasted like heaven. Bob convinced her to boil water to supplement our supply. Unflavored hot water, after a long day in the sweltering sun, was not easy to get down. Still, it was wet ... and safe.

Through such selflessness, starvation wasn't an issue on my many mission trips. I might've gotten hungry and lost weight, but starve? Never happened.

Back at our makeshift camp, I stretched atop my bedroll, exhausted. With a full stomach and satisfied soul, I gazed up at the bright stars hanging majestically in the heavens, the firmament unmarred by electric lights. A shooting star trailed across the Milky Way as my eyelids became heavy and fluttered closed. I slept untroubled by my insomnia.

A chorus of crowing cocks broke the stillness of early dawn. Half-awake, I slowly focused on the dark silhouette of a scantily dressed native staring down at me. Startled, I blurted, "Bob, wake up! We've got company!"

He rolled over with a sleepy grin. "Don't worry, Doc. They all look fierce when you're half-asleep." He then mumbled, "*Un momento, señor.*" The villager hesitantly replied in what sounded like broken Spanish.

"He wants to know if we're hungry."

"Well ... I know I am."

"His woman is cooking breakfast right now. We'd better get going." Bob stood and brushed himself off.

I wondered if the woman—a politically incorrect moniker —was the young man's wife, live-in, or something else. *Bob's been in the jungle too long.* We found her scrambling a pan of eggs over an open fire. She added various peppers and herbs, standard fare and good sustenance. I was wide awake after drinking her rocket-fuel coffee.

Although I was a little sore from sleeping on the ground, a clear sky promised a bright and beautiful day, perfect for extracting teeth outside. I had started to pull supplies from my duffle when a group of men arrived with pack mules. They'd begun their trek down the mountain before dawn when it was dangerously dark, determined to take my clinic to their village. They saw me unpacking and frantically loaded our stuff onto their burros.

A small donkey with a wooden saddle was provided for me. Without my having to kick him, he joined the caravan that slowly wound through Usila's dusty lanes. We soon entered a steep, jungle trail that anxiously rose from the valley. It became one of the most grueling treks I'd ever negotiated.

Although the animals were sure-footed, Bob and I dismounted and walked when the trail became overly treacherous, sometimes clambering hand over hand. I'm not sure how the donkeys made it, weighed down by our supplies, but they somehow negotiated narrow ledges along the steep cliffs. Alimony, my high-strung thoroughbred, would've plunged to depths unseen.

The canopy thinned as we climbed ever higher. Noon arrived, and the sun blazed. When my canteen ran low, our guides offered to refill it but I was afraid of contamination.

"It'll be okay," Bob reassured me as he gave his water bottle to an Indian. "Better than dying of thirst."

"That's not very comforting," I muttered while handing my canteen to a porter, who then disappeared into the brush. When he returned about fifteen minutes later, I cautiously sipped to wet my parched lips. It was cold ... and tasty.

"This is great!" I said.

Apparently, the high mountain springs were safe from pollutants. I guzzled it.

At this point our breakfast calories burned low and I was losing steam. Bob called a halt. "Let's rest and have lunch."

"What do we have?" I asked, "I'm starved." Despite having ridden a good part of the way, I was also exhausted.

"Nothing ... yet." Bob plopped into the shade of a small shrub and pulled his hat over his eyes. I leaned against a sapling, twirled a sprig of grass in my mouth, and dozed off.

Soon, the bushes rustled and an Indian emerged with a bunch of bananas. They were small and mottled but had a pleasant fruity taste, unlike anything in our Maryland grocery stores. I gobbled three of them.

We continued along rocky crags, through patches of steamy jungle, and finally up to a fertile plateau where we stopped for a breather. A parade of peaks punctuated the purple horizon in the distance, reminding me of Appalachia, only much hotter.

I hopped onto my burro, happy to be riding again, and we soon entered a small village. Sweaty and grungy, I felt like some unsavory character in a spaghetti Western. Astride the small burro, my feet almost touched the ground. Maybe I looked more comical, like Sancho Panza.

We wound single file through narrow lanes lined by thatched-roof huts, many perched precariously on the over-hanging cliffs. Folks bustling through their daily activities stopped to gawk while romping kids who'd never seen white guys before crowded around. Even mules craned their necks and brayed.

Clothing was similar to that in other villages, except the antediluvian look was more prevalent. Brightly patterned homespun, worn mainly by matriarchs, gave the town a festive air. Several adolescent girls wore modern dresses gifted by doting fathers, but they ran home to don the colorful tradi-tional apparel made by their mothers. They proudly modeled them but soon took them off in favor of lightweight cotton. The heavy wraps were hot.

"*Mucho calor!*"

"*Sí.*"

"Very hot" was a common greeting, even at this altitude.

Like a lone sentinel on the high edge of town, a small mission house overlooked the village. After the young, unmarried pastor graciously relinquished his modest hut for our sleeping quarters, Bob took one look inside the dark, musty shack and declared, "How 'bout you and me sleep outside, *amigo*?"

"Sounds good," I agreed. "Would it be okay to drag those two cots out?" I figured they might discourage the night vermin from crawling on me.

Without responding, Bob grabbed one and I snagged the other.

After unpacking our bedrolls, we clambered down the steep hillside to a hovel perched on a ledge where a meal waited. Although it was meager, the owners were happy to share.

We thanked them for their hospitality and trudged up to our cots. Completely spent from the day's trek, I plopped onto mine, ready to turn in. A village chieftain approached and exchanged idle pleasantries with Bob, until he finally got to the point.

Bob turned toward me. "You need to pull a tooth ... tonight."

"Why tonight? It's almost dark."

"An old man traveled days to see you and had to wait when we didn't show up on time."

"I can't work in the dark, Bob. And I'm bushed."

A wizened old guy shuffled over to the head honcho, who insisted that I treat the wandering ancient immediately. For some mysterious reason, he had to return home at first light. Bob offered a compromise.

"You could operate at dawn, after you've rested."

It came down to pulling it in the dark that night or in the dark the next morning. I opted to get it over with.

In the dim light of Bob's beat-up penlight, I rummaged through my duffle bag for a syringe and forceps. It was too late to find a chair, so the patient stood while I injected him. Shaking with nervous exhaustion, I manipulated the tooth while Bob urgently prodded, "Hurry up, Dr. C. The batteries are about to give out."

I'M about to give out, I thought.

When it finally pulled free, I fell onto my cot, relieved. The old man's frail wife, whom I hadn't noticed before, sauntered up and patted his arm.

"She has one that hurts and needs to be pulled," Bob quietly announced. I wondered if he had waited to tell me that.

I went straight to work on her but became desperate as the pathetic flashlight faded. A match would have been brighter. Her tooth came out just as the batteries died. I would've hung out a "Closed" sign if we'd had one.

The osteoporotic grandmother—or possibly great-grandmother—rummaged through her pack and produced a brown egg that she placed in my hand, gently closing my fingers around it. It was one of the most meaningful payments I'd ever received.

The twinkling firmament faintly outlined the couple's bent silhouettes as they slowly disappeared into the black of night. I wondered from whence they had come and to what they were returning.

A verse crossed my mind: "Whatever you do for the least of these, you do for me."

I collapsed onto the crude cot, a mere foot off the ground, and drifted into a deep slumber. I was awakened by the quintessential alarm clock—crowing roosters—refreshed for a day that promised a steady stream of patients. Bob and I set up our clinic under a large shade tree, and he managed to commandeer one of the few chairs in the village.

After another long day of bending over untold numbers, my aching back welcomed the lengthening shadows. Bob organized a cleanup crew and directed me to a patch of grass under another shade tree. "Have a lie-down, Dr. C."

While I snoozed against the trunk, a handsome young lad

around Joel's age—about six at the time—boldly approached and tugged on my hand. Startled, I hopped up. He smiled and gestured to follow. He held my hand while taking me on a tour of his village, speaking in *Chinentaco* while pointing out various landmarks, obviously proud of his town.

When I finally responded, in English, he paused and stared up at me with his big brown eyes. As if on cue, we both broke into a fit of laughter. At that moment, the linguistic barrier wasn't a serious problem.

I pointed to my camera, then to him, indicating that I wanted to take his picture. He proudly posed on a small rope bridge over a deep ravine. I'll never forget his smile. I thought of Joel, Tara, Russell, and Kate, so very far away in both distance and time. A tear trailed down my dirty, sunburnt cheek. My diminutive tour guide waved good-bye and joined his friends who were playing something that looked like ring around the rosy.

That evening, Bob set up his generator, hung a single light bulb from a tree limb, and fired it up. The kids danced around it, never having seen electricity. Bob also brought a projector and showed an inspirational film on a wall. The moving pictures mesmerized everyone in the village, not just the kids.

That night, dinner was a bowl of watery corn meal with three morsels of boiled chicken and a few tiny peas. Seated on the hut's dirt floor, I glanced around and noticed that our portions were larger than anyone else's.

For I was hungered, and ye gave me meat; I was thirsty, and ye gave me drink; I was a stranger, and ye took me in …. Genuine hospitality.

Around midnight, the mayor informed us that we'd have to leave before dawn; a land dispute with surrounding villages had turned ugly. Although the mountain passes were blocked by armed, feuding tribesmen, both sides agreed that we could go if we did so early and without guides. Bob and I quickly packed and began to feel our way down the dark mountain. One of our porters stood at the lower edge of the village and waved good-bye. "*Vaya con Dios, amigos.*" Miraculously, we never got lost.

All too soon, I was winging my way home to Maryland, wondering if the dispute ever became violent. I knew it was the peasants who would suffer the most.

The panorama of mountain peaks soared above a lazy mist in the cool morning air. Kids played unfamiliar games passed down through generations. I thought of the gift of a hot tortilla peeled from the rounded wall of an ancient clay oven. Although I'd gone to help folks like my forebears on Nealy Ridge, I returned the enriched one. The intense jungle heat paled next to the warmth of the people. I fell in love with the work and the missionaries, but most of all with the villagers— plain hill folk, salt of the earth.

Kate can ride a horse. She adores children. Maybe she'll come along next time …

CHAPTER EIGHT

Choral Camping

When I returned from Mexico, Kate met me at the
airport and asked what I most wanted.

"A long hot shower and an ice-cold glass of milk."

After arriving home, I hopped out of the shower and was immediately greeted with my request.

Kate gave me a big hug, then stepped back with a queried look. "You need another shower," she said before I'd even toweled off.

Not only did I reek, Kate still had to put up with something else: my foray into the jungle hadn't cured me of snoring.

Anti-snoring appliances come in all shapes, sizes, and colors. Occasionally it's the wife who snores, but more often the culprit is the husband. At his six-month check-up, he might wait for the pretty hygienist to exit the room before asking, "Oh, by the way, Doc ... before I forget ... it never really bothers me, but ..."

The appliances range from expensive to exorbitant. Many are unreliable and most folks simply hate wearing them, but the spouse often persists, saying, "Look, you've gotta do something about that ungodly racket. I need to get some sleep."

From personal experience, the most effective cure had been a swift jab from my wife's elbow, which often solved the problem, at least for a while. Or maybe it just made her feel better.

But I couldn't use an elbow on the burly guy I was paired to sleep with in a pup tent.

Our son Joel joined the Pyleton Cub Scouts in first grade and proudly strutted around our farm in his orange and black T-shirt. It was hard to get it off him long enough to be washed. Determined, he steadily advanced through the ranks: Bobcat, Wolf, and Bear. I volunteered to help the Pack with various mundane tasks, such as driving rambunctious kids to outings and making sure they didn't kill themselves—or anyone else.

After achieving the Arrow of Light, Cub Scout's highest award, Joel crossed over to Boy Scouts. One of his first meetings ended with an older boy's Eagle ceremony, a solemn candlelit ritual that celebrated his accomplishments and good deeds. Joel turned to me and whispered. "Dad, I want to become an Eagle Scout."

Joel was subsequently elected leader of the Tiger Patrol. Chuck, Pyleton's dedicated scoutmaster, informed me that I was now the parent-advisor by default.

"Sure, why not?" I said. *How hard can it be to herd a bunch of adolescents?*

In light of the rugged mission trips I had taken, Chuck asked me to develop the Troop's High Adventure program. He didn't realize that I sometimes pressed the limits and that that's what kids loved. He, however, was the opposite. Case in point: He once called off a ski trip because it was snowing.

"The roads are slick," he said.

"But it's barely coming down, Chuck. You can't ski without snow!"

"Well, better safe than sorry."

Chuck was the yin to my yang, which was probably a good thing. I could be a little nuts. Kate advised folks who went on foreign missions with me, "If my maniac husband says 'Follow me,' quickly turn around and go the other way."

A proactive scoutmaster, Chuck soon enrolled several Pyleton parents in an eight-week program called Scoutmaster Fundamentals (SMF). The intense training helped me appreciate the responsibility I had assumed for these youngsters' formative years.

Assigned to eight-man patrols, we covered every aspect of scouting, including a good dose of citizenship. During SMF, we had to conquer the same hurdles and pass the same tests as the boys; the training could be grueling for adults who were beginning to experience bodily creaks and aches. But helping to raise up the next generation, all the while having fun, was a reward unto itself. Because of our leader's devotion, I developed a tremendous respect for the Boy Scouts.

The intensity of the four-hour evening workshops paled in comparison to the three-day wilderness campout. For that grand finale, another Pyleton leader, Dwayne, became my tent-mate. The first night it rained—hard—with thunder and lightning beyond all reason. Dwayne and I hunkered down in a pup tent designed for a couple of small boys. Or maybe a man and his dog, but not two beefy men.

I usually slept rather well during a storm, finding an archaic comfort in knowing I wasn't directly exposed to it. The plinking of rain on the copper roof of our bedroom's bay window lulled me into a deep slumber. When camping, I might've put too much faith in those thin nylon walls.

Rain apparently affected Dwayne the same way because he slept like a log, his somnolent snoring competing favorably with the thunder. Our second night was star-filled, so he had no accompaniment for his nocturnal rumblings. For the sake of Beaver Patrol harmony, I decided *not* to suggest that Dwayne get a Snore Guard; I could survive two nights in cramped quarters with my cacophonous roommate.

Despite my sleep deprivation, the SMF weekend turned out to be fun and rewarding.

Some months later, during a regular meeting at which our troop made plans for summer camp, my erstwhile tent-mate strolled over and announced, "Hi, roomy!"

Roomy? For a whole week? "Sure, Dwayne. It'll be great ... just like old times."

I tried to sound enthusiastic, but deep down I wasn't. While Dwayne was salt of the earth, he could no more control his bodily eruptions while asleep than anyone else. And I'm talking about *all* bodily emissions. I bought earplugs—good, expensive ones.

Chuck, several assistant scoutmasters, a handful of dads, and one mom accompanied over fifty boys to Heritage Scout Camp, which was a big turnout. It was a good thing Chuck was good at recruiting adults.

The parents pitched their tents far from the kids, not wanting to be any closer to them than they wanted to be near us. To set an example for the boys, we established a military-straight row at the high end of the campsite, but it didn't matter—the kids' tents ended up helter-skelter. As the head scoutmaster, Chuck positioned his tent at an angle between the boys and the adults to keep an eye on both groups.

During drop-off on the first day, amidst a teeming crowd of tearful parents and chattering Scouts, Dwayne grinned and announced, "Hey, Carroll! I got our tent picked out, right over there." I returned his grin, thinking about my new earplugs. The Scout motto was *Be Prepared*. Although I knew Dwayne would spout forth like Old Faithful, I was confident I'd sleep well.

Stupid me—that first night I forgot to dig out my earplugs, and I wasn't reminded until Dwayne drifted off. At first, I heard a little light snoring floating softly through the dark, barely perceptible, the way Dvořák opened his *New World Symphony*. The prelude was followed by a deep base that resonated in the evening stillness. The sleeping maestro soon reached a crescendo, his nocturnal rumblings as thunderous as I remembered. After a brief intermission, Dwayne began again.

After the first movement, I found the earplugs and inserted them, but Dwayne's snoring penetrated anyway; I might as well have left them at home. *Now what?*

While organizing my gear earlier, I'd noticed an unoccupied tent. Exhausted, I gathered my sleeping bag and duffle and left Dwayne to his loud slumber. Emerging from the tent flap into the stark shadows, I hesitated while getting my bearings, then trudged uphill through the black of night.

"Ouch! Damn it!" I blurted, stubbing my toe against a root. I was afraid that a kid might've heard my un-Scout-like expletive before I realized it was probably drowned out by the deep rumblings broadcast from all the adults. Dwayne wasn't alone in his nocturnal emissions. It was a wonder anyone got any sleep.

Apparently, I was the only one who couldn't. Everyone was sawing wood, including the boys.

After listening to the various discharges for a few minutes, so incongruous with the chirping of a sleeping forest, I also noticed that the crisp pine scent of the woods had been supplanted.

Surprisingly, Dwayne wasn't the loudest; another team member held that honor. After tossing my bedroll onto a newly claimed cot, I further explored to find out who was the loudest of the loud. The champ was sleeping in the angle between the two rows of tents: Chuck, our beloved scoutmaster. I was thankful that my fresh abode was farther from his tent than the one Dwayne had staked out.

THE WHOLE TOOTH

A fairly good night's sleep was the upshot. The following morning, Dwayne looked a little hurt that I'd moved out but cheered up when I told him, "Chuck's snoring is the loudest I've ever heard."

Later in the week, one of the more juvenile adults took a midnight stroll with a tape recorder. He stopped in front of each tent and carefully documented his impressions in a log-book:

High pitched.

Gasping like he's gonna die.

Nasal yet deep.

One entry included a prognosis:

A whistle. Might need sinus surgery.

During the troop banquet that fall, he played his recording through a bullhorn, identifying each person by name and tone. The bullhorn wasn't really necessary, but it was a nice touch. He'd also traveled abroad to other unsuspecting campsites. Our troop was definitely the most accomplished.

As the week wore on, there seemed to be less snoring that was less intense. Or maybe I was just getting used to it—except for that of the champ. Chuck couldn't be squelched.

On the second to last night, I crawled from the sack at my usual late hour for a latrine run. Barely awake, I focused on an anomalous shadow looming in the darkness, like a huge stump blocking my way. Illuminated by a pale crescent moon, I realized that it was an animal's hindquarters. *A whitetail deer?*

The buck was hunched low, his head not quite visible. I tiptoed to the side and saw Chuck's tent flaps tied back, which allowed the deer to shove his head inside. Its antlers were hung up in the guy-wires. While our beloved scoutmaster snored peacefully, the rooting buck had fallen in love. He ignored me and continued to focus on the "courting and sparking" going on between them.

That made it unanimous—everyone loved Chuck. He might've had a heart attack if he'd awakened to see Bullwinkle gazing longingly over his big snout. After a time, the lovesick buck finally stepped back, looked up, and glared at me. He pawed the earth a few times and meandered off.

The next morning I told Chuck about his would-be lover. I don't think he believed me, but that night he secured his tent flaps. That didn't stop him, however, from out-snoring the best of them.

Me? I continued my search for the best earplugs in the world. Cost was no object.

Whenever a patient says, "Doc, I've got a snoring problem," I reflect on those nights at summer camp, remembering that recording played at the Scout banquet and envision hitting the play button for my patient. "Does it sound anything like this?"

Dwayne retired to North Carolina, but I swear I can still hear him from afar.

CHAPTER NINE

S n a k e s

Despite being meticulous and clean, Tania wasn't afraid to get dirty, which was a plus because she was always willing to pitch in. When a patient canceled at the last minute, she'd grab a broom or mop and perform menial tasks, unlike Fran, who strictly did her job.

"I'm not highly trained just to be a janitor," Fran once huffed.

Every morning, Tania would clean the restroom when she arrived (maybe she was just used to keeping up on her boys' bathroom), but she drew the line at dealing with insects. In fact, although her family loved to camp, hike, and canoe—anything that involved the outdoors—Tania couldn't stand bugs (which seemed odd because I've never seen a bug-free campsite). She was particularly squeamish about spiders. Whenever one popped out from under the baseboard, a shriek announced the fact.

As screaming in a dental office is not a good thing, I gently told Tania, "Just *quietly* come get me, and I'll take care of it."

The next time, she managed to stay calm ... until I squished it underfoot.

"Aaaagh," she bellowed, as if someone had just died. "Dr. James, I don't believe you killed it."

What'd she expect me to do? Take it to the local zoo?

One fall morning—when myriad creepy crawlies migrate indoors—Tania and Trish teamed up to trap an intruder scurrying across the floor. They placed a plastic cup over it and waited for me to arrive. Anticipating my reaction, they giggled as I nonchalantly picked up the cup, but screeched when I promptly tromped it to death.

"Please don't yell like that. It's not good for business," I said, trying to sound stern. But I don't think I pulled it off.

One of my assistants, Louise, once caught an exceptionally large, hard-shell critter in a similar manner. She carefully scooted a stiff piece of paper under the inverted Solo cup, picked it up, and placed it on my desk. Then she gently removed the paper, leaving the inmate concealed within its prison.

I picked up the cup while she peeked through the door-way. "I see you found my pet tarantula, Louise." Summarily brushing it to the floor, I crunched the "pet" under foot. Louise was usually cool about such things, but I heard a distinct "Yuk" from around the corner.

Springtime in Gloyd invariably found my staff lunching on our back deck, under the shade of an ornamental plum tree. In decided contrast to crawling bugs, Tania was indifferent toward flying intruders, absentmindedly swatting at flies and yellow jackets. She wasn't about to allow such small distractions to spoil the sunshine and fresh air.

One beautiful afternoon, about halfway through our repast, Tania casually chewed a baby carrot while staring off to the side. "Dr. C. What's that stick poking through the deck? It doesn't look big enough to chain a dog."

We'd recently fenced the yard around our new swimming pool, so our dogs were no longer permitted to freely roam the Gloyd countryside. The wooden deck was only a foot or two above ground level, and it often sprouted weeds but no saplings. "Thhick?" I mispronounced through a half-chewed bite.

"That one, right over there, near the pool," she pointed.

I leaned back and saw the stick poking up between the boards, thinking, *Maybe it fell feet-first off the plum tree.* While I reflected, the stick turned its head toward us.

"Snaaaaake," Tania screeched, jumping up and knocking her chair over. In one swift move, she hopped onto an adjacent lawn chair. Her feather weight worked in her favor—the worn, frail netting of the old chair held while she quaked uncontrollably. When the intruder turned its head away, she bent over to grab her lunch and, for some strange reason, mine. Motivated by fear, she leapt from the chair and made a mad dash for the back door. I swear her feet never once touched the ground.

The other gals were fine until Tania split. Panic then spread and they grabbed their own lunches and followed her into the house, gathering behind the safety of the screen door. That left me alone and amused, but without my sandwich. I would've finished it if Tania hadn't taken it. Snakes have never bothered me; rats are a different story. I hate rats and am sure they hate me.

In all the excitement of high-pitched squeals, the snake slithered farther out. Something had to be done or we'd never eat outside again. The whole crew, but especially Tania, needed placating, so I squeezed through the doorway, which was partially blocked, while they kept an eye on the snake. I fetched my BB gun from the hall closet.

Joel came up with the idea of snake shooting while Kate and I were away at a medical mission seminar in North Carolina. A young couple stayed at the house with him over the long weekend: Arnold, a blond, blue-eyed German-American, and Marie Louisa Consuela Shultz, originally from Peru (her full name always struck me as interesting—it just didn't flow).

In her swimsuit, Marie stepped into the warm sunshine with a magazine tucked under one arm and a glass of lemonade in her hand. Finding a small snake curled up on the lounge chair of her choice, she screamed and Joel came running.

He quickly assessed the situation and grabbed my BB gun. Taking careful aim, he put a ball in the reptile's head—first shot, dead center, right between the eyes. Marie retreated to the safety of the great indoors to read her magazine, even though the serpent was out of the picture.

When we returned home from North Carolina, Joel showed me his trophy, which he'd proudly draped over the back fence. He was surprised that Marie had become so unnerved by the whole episode, especially the hunt.

"Just because I'm a high-strung Latino doesn't mean I like slimy, slithery creatures," she declared. "I'm from Lima for crying out loud."

I removed the leathered carcass from the top rail and tossed it into the back field, out of sight.

It was now my turn to eliminate a snake that invaded my backyard. The sight of my BB gun further agitated the ladies.

"What're you gonna do with that?" A look of horror flooded Tania's face.

"Isn't it obvious?" I grinned. That's when I noticed it wasn't your typical black snake. It had bronze markings and a triangular shaped head. *A copperhead!* At that point I knew I had to eliminate the satanic reptile before they realized how deadly it really was.

While working my Red Ryder's pump action, I stalked across the savannah of my pool deck. The women, attired in scrubs, almost swooned at the sight of their mild-mannered dentist challenging the three-foot snake.

"Be careful."

"Don't hurt it."

They didn't want me to kill it in front of them, they just wanted it gone. *If they only knew!*

I closed on my quarry, but not too close. BB guns are inherently inaccurate and my first shot went wild. I felt a little silly not using my air rifle, which was far more accurate and powerful. One step closer brought a second shot ricocheting off the deck. It slammed into the barbecue grill with a distinct, metallic *ping*. But the snake didn't flinch.

"Watch out! You'll shoot your eye out," Tania announced, plagiarizing *A Christmas Story*. She seemed more concerned about my safety than my wife did, but then again Kate's accustomed to my doing stupid things.

Yet another shot missed the mark.

"A little to the left." Behind the screen door, Tania had edged toward the front of the pack. She didn't want me to kill it, but she didn't want it alive either. The fourth shot sped close-by the snake's head, a near miss. It hadn't moved since the assault began.

Everyone got into the spirit of things.

"A little lower."

"No, more to the right."

"Yeah, but still down just a bit."

"Pump it up, good and hard."

Behind the security of a snake-proof screen door, they became almost enthusiastic.

"Make sure you hit it this time."

"Yeah, it's not going to stay still all day."

Determined to avoid embarrassment—after all, Joel got his snake on the first shot—I took a deep breath and slowly squeezed the trigger. *Splat*—square in the head. Blood gushed from the serpent as its partially decapitated body slithered through the planks and disappeared. There was a chorus of yuks, ughs, and oohs from the peanut gallery. Plastered against the screen, the most prominent face of the bunch was Tania's.

Hitching up my pants, I triumphantly strutted back to the house. The ladies opened the door and parted to make way for their hero-hunter. I leaned the gun against our wood stove, which I thought was a nice touch. "Where's my lunch?"

Tania sheepishly pointed to the kitchen table. Despite protests about "that poor snake," everyone had managed to finish their meals. Mine was the lone sandwich remaining.

I wondered how Tania ever survived camping. *She probably uses denial,* I thought, *but doesn't she know snakes are everywhere, even if unseen?*

I decided it best not to tell her.

CHAPTER TEN

Why Birds?
Why Not?

After Tuffy, Russell's first horse, died from traumatic injuries, then Joel's pony Dolly passed from old age, Kate and I decided that boarding horses was a bad idea. Rigor mortis animals lying around the farm wouldn't be a practice builder for my embryonic home office.

On the other hand, Rusty, our mongrel rescue mutt, was good for business. He greeted patients with a slobbery lick, especially targeting those who were leery. Rusty wanted to convert everyone into a dog lover.

"Your filthy animal spit on my hand," one Middle-Eastern patient complained to Kate.

"Be careful," she said, trying to make light of it, "he might lick you to death."

But he bolted for the bathroom and scrubbed for a full ten minutes. He only came to my Rockville office after that.

Most folks adored Rusty, drool and all. Kids brought doggy treats for him and carrots for the horses. We found that pets were soothing for most nervous dental patients. With the ambience of horses, dogs, and cats, I figured: why not expand our menagerie?

Bull was a good ole boy who owned a farm a couple miles up the road. Along with the quintessential cats and dogs, sheep and goats, horses and cattle, pigs and chickens, he raised exotic animals like llamas and peacocks.

His wife, Lanie, provided before- and after-school daycare. She was great with kids, always keeping them busy with outdoor activities. If the weather was inclement, she read to them or had them read to her. Although not licensed, she was excellent with youngsters, far better than many of the suburban nursery factories. When Kate went back to work part-time, Lanie took in Joel, with whom she was already acquainted, even though she usually didn't watch preschoolers.

Bull and Lanie had begun to raise Vietnamese potbelly pigs and naturally, Joel wanted one. But I'd slopped hogs on Nealy Ridge and wanted no part of exotic swine that had to be kept indoors during the winter, so I diverted Joel's attention by asking Bull, "What're your peacocks like?"

"Dumb and purrty, like women."

I let the comment slide. "How do you take care of 'em?"

"Toss out some cracked corn. Easier 'n dogs or cats."

"What do they do?"

"Eat and poop. The boy struts about and the gal lays eggs to make more peacocks. I don't like the taste of 'em—the eggs or the birds," he said with a sly grin. Actually Bull seldom ate his animals, except the pigs and white Leghorn chickens.

"Do they stay close to home?" I asked.

"Only if you keep 'em penned in. They roost inside that pen over there."

I turned to Joel. "What do you think, son?"

A male stopped strutting and spread his tail feathers. Joel smiled and nodded. I shelled out a few bucks for one cock and a hen.

"It'll take three years fer him to reach full plumage," Bull explained. "That's when you can really tell the difference."

I certainly couldn't tell them apart now.

So to house these new family members, I built an eight-foot fence out of chicken wire. About thirty feet in diameter, it encircled a white birch tree that I figured would be good for roosting. After finishing it with a sturdy gate I made from oak boards left over from our fencing project, I was proud of the enclosure. The peacocks were a nice addition to our farmette, and kids waiting for appointments liked chasing them around the outside perimeter.

As Burt and Ernie grew—never mind that one was a girl; Joel watched *Sesame Street* and thus they were named—they began escaping from my aviary. I had no idea how they were getting out, but obviously the fence had quit doing its job. In the morning I'd find them clucking at the gate, trying to get back inside to be fed and watered. If I wasn't up and outside early, they wandered off.

Soon after their first escape, an elderly neighbor phoned. "Come get yer stupid birds. Can't you keep them damn things penned up?"

"Why's he so upset?" I asked Kate.

"I don't know, but you'd better figure out how they're getting out."

When I went to fetch them, I found the old man scraping his deck with a spackling knife. He stood up and straightened his back. "See what your birds did?" He was not a happy camper.

I looked down and saw a pile of crap on his deck, right in front of the sliding glass door. When peacocks see their reflection, they peck at the enemy in the glass. And with every peck, they poop (this gave "bird-brain" a whole new meaning to me). His wife had stepped outside earlier, directly into the fresh pile of guano. Her shoes were leaning against the house, drying in the sun after he'd hosed them off.

Gathering up skittish peacocks wasn't easy. I couldn't catch them, so I ran behind, flailing my arms erratically. It seemed to help if I squawked.

"You look like the village idiot," Kate said, laughing. Herding fugitive fowl was an exercise in public humiliation.

I followed Bull's instructions when making the coop, so what's the problem? I wondered. It was too tall for them to jump over and the birch tree was dead center. Then I discovered that they were roosting on the wooden gate, which was sturdy enough to hold them. At dawn, they'd jump down and land outside the cage.

I told Bull, "I didn't think they could jump as high as the gate."

"They can't. They probably fly up," he suggested.

"I assumed they couldn't fly, like turkeys."

"Ya gotta clip their wings. I guess I forgot to tell ya that." He then explained the fine art of clipping. "Cut off the underneath feathers. They can't fly, an' don't look so bad."

"Both wings?"

Bull chuckled. "Jus' one. Can't fly with only one wing."

Before I had a chance to clip them, Burt and Ernie again flew the coop. I inquired around, but no one had seen them. I was a little suspicious of the old retired guy.

While straddling the barnyard fence a week or so later, treating our horses to cut apples, something caught my eye. Two large birds were flying across our pasture from the far hillside. They picked up speed while bearing down on me and pulled up at the last minute.

Burt landed on Alimony's hindquarters. Ever skittish, he reared and took off in a run. The freaked-out peacocks, not finding a friendly berth, screeched and fluttered about before flying to the forest beyond the hill. After another few days, they returned. I think they missed their supper.

Tara, our eldest, often helped with unusual chores, so one day I asked her, "You want to help clip their wings?"

"I ... I guess," she said. She knew it wasn't really a question. I conveniently neglected to tell her about my dad's run-in with a rooster.

When I was about ten, Dad showed me how to chop off chicken heads. They do run around, or more accurately, flop around. Our birddogs loved chasing them, but my Bantam rooster was pretty upset. He sprang at Dad, flipped his claws up, and stapled my father's legs with his sharp heel spurs, gouging two deep holes above his ankle. Dad cursed as two thin red streams flowed down. It looked seriously painful.

With that experience in mind, I insisted that Tara and I both wear long sleeves, jeans, and heavy gloves while catching our peacocks. I didn't tell her why.

There was no easy way to catch them, so we planned to herd them into the barn. Reluctantly donning her armor, Tara looked around to see if any of her friends were coming up the drive. She would be wholly embarrassed if anyone witnessed my squawking while I chased them. They finally ran inside and Tara slammed the barn door shut.

The next step was to trap one inside a stall where we could grab it. I foolishly dove for one wily fowl and tripped—the peacock easily dodged me. Worse, I landed face down; neither Tara nor Russell had mucked the stalls. It reminded me of the first time I tried to saddle Alimony.

"Tara. Come in here and corner him from the other side." I pointed while still sprawled on the ground.

"No waaay!" she said. I couldn't blame her.

I struggled to my feet and lunged again, but only managed to grasp a handful of short quills. Enveloped in a storm of feathers, and covered in manure, I felt like I'd been tarred and feathered, only I smelled worse. A little angry, at no one in particular, I insisted that Tara join me in the stall.

"Let's try a slower approach," I suggested. As I closed in, Tara stayed off to the side, slowly fanning the air with her arms. When I shouted "Now!" we both dove and slammed our heads together. Although dazed, I somehow managed to grab Burt's leg—I think it was Burt—and then fell back into horse poop.

While lying in the manure, I tucked the peacock under my arm while Tara cut the wing's undersurface with dull kitchen shears. After the jagged clipping, I released him back into the aviary. Ernie gave up without much of a fight.

"That should hold them," I declared.

Early the next morning, I got another call from our retired neighbor. He wasn't happy.

"Are you sure they're ours?" I hadn't looked outside yet.

"Of course. Who the hell else owns birds that wander all over the countryside?"

They were, in fact, AWOL, but he had already chased them off his property, and I couldn't find them anywhere else.

A few days later, Russell spotted them cruising erratically from atop our barn. "It looks like Eddie Rickenbacker, shot to pieces by the Red Baron," Russell said, laughing. We used to watch old war flicks together.

"Yeah, but only if they were trailing black smoke," I said.

"Their wings need to be clipped shorter," he suggested without offering to help.

I was on my own, but surely they would be easier to catch with their wings already clipped.

After a successful trim and the passage of time, Ernie's feathers slowly grew into a kaleidoscope of color. Strutting his stuff, he fanned his plumage to the delight of gawking kids and distracted adults. And they remained in the aviary for a full year.

Despite the challenges with the additions to our brood, Kate always scanned the Sunday classifieds, where animals were inevitably featured.

One day she announced, "A litter of mixed yellow labs was just born in Potomac. Labs are adorable and they're giveaways." She called the number and a pleasant, but formal-sounding lady answered.

"Most are already taken, but a few are left," she said.

That afternoon we drove through a security gate to a large mansion.

"Wow. Look at this place," Joel said, his mouth hanging open.

We were greeted by a wealthy divorcee who sported a row of ugly caps that probably cost a fortune. Her enormous foyer echoed our footsteps as I looked up at a chandelier that might have cost as much as our half-built house. She led us down a long hallway to a laundry room that was bigger than our family room. I could almost read Kate's mind: *Why can't I have a laundry room like this?*

While we handled each pup, the mama Lab eyed us suspiciously from her shag rug bed. One lively little critter followed Joel everywhere. It was a match. Since they were too young to wean, I arranged to pick up Lizzy (Joel had already named her) in a couple of weeks.

On the appointed day, I stopped by after work.

"One pup, a male, has yet to be claimed," the owner said with a frown.

"Well, he shouldn't be left out," I said, smiling.

Grateful to unload them both, she gave a friendly wave from her eight-foot, double front door while I drove out the tree-lined lane. I couldn't wait to get home and show the kids.

I briskly marched up our back walkway with a cute little puppy tucked under each arm. Kate, who loves dogs, was dumbfounded. Joel took Lizzy while Russell, ecstatic to have his own dog, named the boy Sam.

"As long as I don't have to clip anything," was Tara's response.

Rusty, the patriarch, was standoffish, but they soon became

best buddies. Like Rusty, they roamed free (this was prior to the pool). On *rare* occasions I allowed the two siblings inside.

Hazel, my friend Stan's wife from New Jersey, raised pedigree show dogs, and she stopped by one day to meet our new puppies on her way to Richmond.

"Carroll, you're an idiot," she said. "Littermates are nothing but trouble."

She was right. Sam and Lizzy proved to be no exception.

Every year, we purchased Christmas lights after December 25th to take advantage of the great deals. After a few years, our Gloyd home was ablaze for the holidays. The Christmas after adopting Sam and Lizzy, Kate and I returned from a holiday party and found our house cloaked in darkness. *Maybe a tripped circuit?*

I went straight to the basement and found that all the breakers were working. Then I went outside to investigate and tripped over something in the darkness. As my eyes adjusted, I saw that it was an extension cord, but only a six-foot section—both ends were frayed.

I retrieved a flashlight and discovered innumerable orange fragments scattered throughout the yard. Interspersed were dozens of short green wires with little decorative lights. Our miscreant littermates had chewed everything into irreparable bits.

Livid at Kate's puppies—now they were *her* dogs—I chased them around the property while ranting and raving. At one point, Kate heard me trip and fall.

"Are you okay, Carroll?" she shouted.

I can't repeat exactly what I said, but she was relieved when I couldn't catch them.

Every summer, while weeding our flower beds, I continued to find archaeological evidence of a Christmas past.

The following spring was unseasonably chilly. One night, I awoke with a start upon hearing a loud cry.

"Help ... help!"

My heart pounded as I flew out of bed to investigate. The bloodcurdling plea came from outside. I flipped on the flood-lights and peeked through the curtains on our sliding glass door.

Kate tiptoed up. "Do you see anything?"

Not hearing her, I jumped. "Nothing. I'm going outside to check it out."

"Be careful," she whispered.

I slipped out the kitchen door and slowly worked my way into the far shadows but found nothing amiss. The multiple pleas had mysteriously ceased as soon as I stepped outside. Believing that I'd disrupted some foul play, I turned toward the house, only to be blinded by the floodlights.

"Hey, Kate. Turn those suckers off. I can't see a thing."

When they went out, I saw nothing but spots. I blinked and glanced up at our roof. On the peak, two dark silhouettes were outlined by a pale moon that peeked through the clouds. Curious, I stared at the apparitions until I heard another cry for "Help." That was echoed by another one. I snarled, "Burt and Ernie."

Stark against the eerie haze of the emerging moon, they made great targets. *My .22 hangs over the mantel*, I thought. I shook my head to clear my brain. *Nah, probably just shoot a hole in the roof.*

As a result of their incessant escapes, Tara and I had to clip their wings even shorter. But until we could do so, they made a habit of roosting over Russell's bedroom. He hated their nocturnal cry.

The Gloyd office was open on select Saturdays, and as Tania worked her tail off in hygiene, I saw numerous emergency drop-ins. It was always a nonstop parade of patients.

On one bustling Saturday in early autumn, a few passing drizzles accentuated the gloominess of the sky. Unfortunately, lousy weather and dark clouds tend to intensify a patient's dread of the dentist.

Around midmorning, I was briskly walking to the next operatory when Kate pulled me into my private office. In a low, anxious tone she said, "Everyone's talking about something nauseating outside. They're all grossed out."

According to waiting room scuttlebutt, *my* dogs—those vagabonds now belonged only to me—were feeding on the bloody remains of some dead animal. Our driveway had become a theater of the macabre; folks driving up had front row seats for the carnivorous banquet.

"You need to go check it out—and I mean right now!" Kate admonished.

"I don't have time," I half-whispered through gritted teeth. "We're way behind because of the emergencies you squeezed in."

Without another word, we went back to work. After the last patient left, I immediately threw my raincoat on and went outside to see what *Kate's* mutts were up to.

I walked down the driveway as the last car turned onto Stabletown Road. An incredible stench hung thickly in the humid air as all three dogs lay prone around a hunk of carrion. Undiscouraged by swarming flies, Sam, Lizzy, and Rusty contentedly chewed, their bellies already distended. Like in *The Far Side*, this slaughterhouse scene would've been complete if they'd had checkered napkins tied around their necks.

The dogs didn't even pause to look at me. Their buffet consisted of one foreleg, shoulder, neck, and head with an eight-point rack. *Why'd they drag it home?* They got sick to their stomachs, so I wouldn't let them into the house, despite the rain. For once, Kate agreed with me.

Another memorable Saturday dawned bright and sunny, accented by a crisp blaze of late autumn color. Myriad patients filed nonstop into the waiting room, chatting about some brightly colored feathers scattered along our lane:

"It's quite pretty, the way the wind swirls the leaves and feathers together."

"Yes. The dogs are having a blast romping through them. One has a feather stuck in his mouth."

"My child took a couple of them."

"Where did all those lovely feathers come from, anyway?"

I had a sinking feeling. *Why must those mongrels eat their prey in front of patients?*

As soon as work ended, I stormed out of the office and found Kate's mutts—again, they were hers—prancing around the parking lot with trophy feathers dangling from their slobbery mouths.

Kate followed me outside and stepped between me and the dogs as I was about to knock the pride right out of them.

"Carroll," she said. "You have birddogs and you have birds. You have to make a choice."

I agreed. My anger ebbed as I realized that they were a reflection of my own mischievous adolescence. There was no contest between man's best friend and a few dim-witted birds.

In the course of one short week, the peacocks—I'd gotten several more—slowly disappeared. Once the dogs had sampled one, they gobbled the whole lot. As with a bag of potato chips, they couldn't stop at just one.

If you visited our home during that time, you might've noticed the faint outline of an abandoned aviary. Yes, I chose birddogs and never regretted it. Besides, Kate moved on to sheep, and lucky for all of us—the patients included—the dogs only chased them for sport.

CHAPTER ELEVEN

The RV

C ut off by an erratic driver, I swerved hard and sideswiped a curb to avoid hitting a car. The cabinet doors flew open, spewing cans and cereal boxes. Cornflakes scattered across the threadbare carpet.

Frank, Kate's dad, yelled, "What the hell are you doing? Trying to get us all killed?"

"Did you want me to hit him?" I shouted back.

I cut the wheel and the RV tilted, swinging the cabinet doors shut. The refrigerator door, improperly latched, flew open and launched a carton of milk. The top burst open and covered the strewn cereal with milk. Tara and Russell giggled uncontrollably in my rearview mirror.

Eyeing them, I didn't see the speed bump, and a carton of eggs bounced from the open frig and landed with a sickening crunch. *Why the eggs?* At the same time, Tara's jewelry flew off a countertop and splashed into the goo spreading across the carpet. "Stop driving so crazy, Daddy," she demanded. She wasn't laughing now.

"I didn't try to hit the bump."

"She's right, slow down," Frank bellowed.

I looked at the speedometer. "We're doing 38 in a 40."

"Keep your eyes on the road," Frank growled.

"Slow down, Dad," Tara pleaded while Russell continued to grin.

"Are you deaf? I'm *not* speeding."

Kate squeezed between the front swivel seats. "Quiet," she snapped. "If you can't get along, I'll drive."

"Let's pull over, clean up this mess, and start over." Jean, Kate's mom, was the voice of reason.

I turned into a JC Penney parking lot and hit a pothole, which further stirred the carpet omelet. Jean quickly cleaned up and stowed anything salvageable while Kate threw the rest into a dumpster. I wrapped a bungee cord across the refrigerator door and securely latched the cabinets.

When I started to climb back into the captain's chair, Frank snarled, "How 'bout I drive, hotshot?" He bowled past me and sat behind the truck-like steering wheel. Kate glared at us while Jean diplomatically gazed out the side window.

"Okay," I acquiesced.

Frank hit the same pothole on his way out. I smiled.

Back on the road, things looked completely different from the passenger seat. As we drifted from side to side, I leaned out my window. "Watch out! You're too close."

"Not as close as you. You hit the damn curb."

"Oh yeah?"

"Stop it!" Kate shouted. "You sound like a couple of kids. One more word and I'm driving."

"Yes, dear." I glanced back. Tara was grinning again; she'd cleaned her bracelet and latched it safely around her wrist. Russell was immersed in his Game Boy.

Frank stared straight ahead. We finally reached the interstate where the drainage ditch was deep enough to swallow us whole if we drifted too far. My palms sweated, but I kept my tongue.

∞

It had all started two months prior when Jean's family began planning their triennial Arkansas reunion. I looked forward to the pickin'-n-strummin', which brought back memories of Nealy Ridge. Frank and I were both strapped for cash; I had gone back to school for orthodontics, and Frank had just retired. He knew a guy, who knew a guy, whose second cousin leased rent-a-wreck RV's. "We'll save thirty percent," he announced.

"Perfect," I agreed. We split the cost.

To get an early start, Frank fetched it from northern Virginia while Kate, Tara, Russell, and I headed to his house in our packed Pinto wagon. We were excited until we saw the ugly rust and primer-gray scratched and dented pile of junk in Frank's driveway. No two tires matched, except all were equally bald. One side window featured a long, trailing crack. The windshield was intact, but not the dry-rot wiper blades.

Frank walked around the corner with a bag of groceries. "So, what do you think?" he proudly beamed.

"Little small, isn't it?"

"Nah. Sleeps six, gets great mileage. We're splitting it fifty-fifty, so you're coming out ahead with four people," he said with a wink. "Come inside. It's nicer than it looks."

My head banged the low doorway as the screen door slammed my butt, a wire stabbing me. The screen's large holes wouldn't even discourage flying vermin on steamy Southern nights. (We later discovered that the A/C didn't work and placed duct tape over those holes.) A couple of dim bulbs lit the musty interior, which smelled of a hint of sewage. The ragged paisley curtains almost covered the small windows.

The kitchen was defined by a two-burner gas range with one cabinet above and one next to it. The dwarf refrigerator and small countertop sat opposite the stove. A postage-stamp table sported two vinyl benches, each torn and big enough for only one and a half people. The door to the toilet/shower/sink was cleverly disguised as wall paneling; that was the only sink onboard.

Above the pilot and copilot seats was a miniscule berth with a two-foot clearance. At the far end, down a narrow hallway, hung a paisley curtain that matched the window dressings. It hid the double bed that Frank and Jean would literally have to crawl into. There was one tiny nightstand whose reading light didn't work, even with a new bulb.

I whacked my head again on the way out. Rubbing it, I asked, "Hey, Frank. Where do we all sleep?"

"The table converts into a double—that's for you and Kate. Both kids can sleep in that berth above the driver." It was pretty small, and Tara was developing into a twelve-year-old adolescent, so I shuddered at her reaction to sleeping like sardines with her brother.

"Let's load up and hit the road," I said, not wanting to dwell on the accommodations.

We quickly stocked the cabinets with groceries and jammed luggage where we could. The kids piled their schoolwork helter-skelter on the counter. We forced the dresser drawers shut under the bench seats, which later protected our clothes from the floor omelet. I stowed my quintessential daypack in front of the suicide seat.

After the aforementioned altercation, Frank and I learned that driving an RV is more like piloting a boat. We settled into the gentle sway while we traveled up the Shenandoah Valley, along the Blue Ridge Mountains, proclaimed one of the most beautiful spots on earth by *National Geographic*.

Many of the settlers of the fertile land were of German heritage. Industrious people, their picturesque farms produced food and forage that fed the ragged Confederate armies. Although many were pacifists, they were caught in the middle of a brutal conflict that destroyed their homes and farms.

The Valley had again become an oasis of pastoral serenity, except when Frank and I got into it.

"Move over. Stop hogging the left lane," I'd say.

"I'm passing that guy," Frank would counter.

"What guy?"

"The guy we just passed."

"It's my turn to drive."

"I'm fine. Go see what the girls are up to." Frank would turn to glare and then swerve.

"They're right here, and watch where you're going."

After seven hours, we passed the Abingdon exit, which led to Mom's ancestral home. I quietly reminisced about summers on Nealy Ridge while Tara and Russell supposedly worked on their schoolwork. They were actually wrestling on Jean's bed.

"Are you guys doing any homework?" I asked.

Russell proudly announced, "Mine's all done!"

"That's great, buddy," I said.

Later, after we arrived in Arkansas, I found out he really hadn't finished it. But this was their vacation too, so despite receiving schoolwork in advance, I understood their desire to goof off. *Maybe on the ride home*, I reasoned.

Ten or twelve hours into the expedition, we approached Nashville, and tensions again flared while we searched for a KOA. For some reason, we ended up downtown even though campgrounds were usually on the outskirts. I tried to maneuver through the narrow streets, but it was hard to do.

"You're gonna hit a curb ... again," Frank shouted.

Kate leaned forward and stared him down. He lowered his voice and suggested we stop and ask for directions.

"Who are we going to ask—that guy peeing against the wall?" I said.

While I stirred up more trouble, the kids plastered their faces against the window to see the guy.

"We're lost, and in a bad part of town," Frank said, pointing out the obvious. "*Now* do you want me to drive?"

"I'm doing fine, Frank. You keep a lookout."

"A lookout for what, another guy taking a wiz?"

The RV bounced off another evil curb.

"Yeah, Carroll, you're doin' just great!"

Kate's face turned bright red, just as I saw signs to the interstate. Then darkness approached at sixty miles per hour. "I can't find the headlights," I said, fumbling around the dashboard.

Frank reached across me. "They're right there next to the wheel."

I swerved. "Get your arm back. You're going to get us killed."

"Well then, turn the lights on."

I pulled the knob and the windshield wipers flipped on. I turned it and the dome light lit. Then I found the emergency flashers. *At least no one will run into us.* I groped for anything to pull, turn, or push, and suddenly the headlamps sprang to life. Well, one anyway, its glorious beam immediately illuminating a sign that read:

KOA
100 yards ahead on the right

The kids were out the door before our tenement-on-wheels rolled to a complete stop. They disappeared into the camp store, craving junk food.

Frank grumbled, "Hope they still have an RV hookup." He went into the rustic cabin with a burnt-wood sign that proudly proclaimed Camp Office and soon emerged with a site map. "Last one. It's pretty far from the showers and toilets."

Kate and her Mom looked skeptical.

"I'll navigate," Frank said. The lane was dark and he actually wanted me to drive. With only one beam to light our way, I managed to whack off a couple tree limbs.

"If it's not a curb, it's a tree," said Frank with a huff.

"Just tell me where to turn."

"Make a left here."

"Where?"

"Right here!"

"This is just a footpath." I didn't think the RV would make it.

"Look, there's the sign."

Frank was right. *Banjo Lane.* I scraped a few more branches while negotiating the tight turn.

"Slow down. Our spot's right here."

Slow down? We were barely moving.

An enormous house on wheels was parked in the next hookup over. I inched into our spot and hit the brakes, which screeched, deafening in the quiet of the woods. The kids piled out before I turned the engine off. I offered to connect the water and electric so the ladies could rustle up some chow.

"The stove doesn't work," Kate announced.

"Neither does the refrigerator," Jean echoed. She held up the warm hamburger meat—it didn't look appetizing. She tossed it and we settled on PB&J with warm soda from the busted refrigerator. Even with everyone famished, the simple meal lifted our spirits. Afterwards, the kids busied themselves with whatever kids do around campsites.

Frank wandered over to meet the neighbors, a retired couple in lawn chairs enjoying the cool evening air. Their awning ran the full length of their large RV. I had cranked ours open to discover the canvas long gone; only a few shards hung on the corroded frame.

"Nice RV," Frank complemented them. "Seems your mobile home is over twice as long as ours. I like the bump-outs. How many does it sleep?"

The old guy smiled and glanced at his wife. "Two."

"How far do you have to go?" she asked.

"Another ten-hour day," Frank replied.

The man noticed that we had six people crammed into our

tiny rig. "Well, good luck. Hope ya'll are still talkin' at the end."

Frank returned and sat in a camp chair next to Kate, Jean, and me while we made plans.

"How 'bout hitting the road early and getting to Opryland when it opens?" I suggested.

"Sounds good," Frank agreed.

The serenity of a forest at night had eased tensions, and exhaustion had set in.

"I'm going to take a quick shower and hit the sack," Kate announced.

"Me too," Jean said.

When Kate yanked the screen door to open it, it fell off one hinge.

"I'll give it a quick fix while you get ready for bed," I said, managing a half-smile.

I quickly discovered that the screws were rusted, so I broke the other hinge loose and leaned the door against a tree where it remained, duct tape and all, when we pulled out the next morning.

Kate ran the shower for a long time before bellowing, "There's no hot water."

"I'll look for a breaker," I said. But I couldn't find one. In searching for it, though, I stepped in a puddle of water; the carpet was soaked. We wouldn't be taking any showers—hot or cold—in the RV. The kids didn't care, but Kate, Jean, and Frank didn't see it that way.

"You know, there's a nice hot shower down that lane," I pointed.

The ladies stared into the darkness and announced in unison, "No way." Kate had no intention of trekking through a spooky tunnel of trees to communal facilities and neither did Jean.

In the meantime, I tried to find the leak. I soon found out that it wasn't just from the shower; the toilet also leaked—big time. There was no choice: everyone had to use the public bathrooms.

"I'll walk you down," Frank offered, disappearing down the ambling lane with the gals in tow. After evening ablutions, they felt much better.

While they cleaned up, I arranged the kids' bed and took them to the toilets. This is when Tara realized that she'd have to share the narrow bunk with her younger brother. "That's not fair!" she said, stomping.

I eyeballed the cramped space on the converted kitchen table where Kate and I were supposed to bed down.

"So, Russell," I ventured, "how 'bout you and I sleep outside?"

"Okay, Dad."

He was a camper at heart, like me, and the solitude sounded good. We flung our bedrolls on the ground and enjoyed a night under the stars while the others slept within. Tara was happy to have a private cubbyhole. Despite a few bumps in the road, literally, things were sorting themselves out.

To get an early start, Russell and I rose with the sun. He sat up, rubbed his eyes, and grumbled. "I'm sore from sleeping on the ground."

"Yeah. Me, too."

That set the tone for the day.

Hearing us, Tara said. "Why do we have to get up so early? We're supposed to be on vacation."

"Just ten more minutes, please!" Kate yelled, an unusual request for her.

Opryland would have to wait.

Frank was an early riser and nowhere to be seen, but his familiar voice floated through the mist from across the way. The retired couple had already given him a mug of joe. Jean wasn't her spry self, but she volunteered to hike up to the camp store for hot coffee for the rest of us. We all needed at least one cup. And as we'd managed to salvage some cereal, Jean purchased a small carton of whole milk too. That would have to do for breakfast.

"Yuk. This is awful," Tara announced.

"There's no skim milk. It bit the dust yesterday," I reminded her.

Camp breakfast was a bust, but Denny's was a hit.

And Opryland was a welcome reprieve from our life in a decrepit RV.

The kids had a blast riding log flumes, roller coasters, and a steam train that was held up by bandits. They semi-enjoyed the bluegrass/hillbilly shows we dragged them to. After a full day at Opryland, we were exhausted when we hit the road at sundown.

After another KOA, another night without a private shower, another stiff-backed morning, the kids were beginning to stink.

"Whew. I haven't smelled anything like this since army days," Frank exclaimed.

"First thing ya'll are gonna do when we git to the reunion is bathe." Jean's Arkansas accent bubbled to the surface as we inched ever closer to the Mississippi River.

Breakfast was fast food, and after making good time, we stopped for lunch at another similar joint—back-to-back gourmet meals. Maneuvering our rusted hulk through a narrow archway was scary, and of course Frank had more to say about my driving. But I did manage without taking the building down ... or even hitting it.

Late that afternoon, we arrived at Aunt Peggy's home in the beautiful Ozarks. There were hugs for all, including Tara and Russell, who were Kate's stepkids. Though no one said anything about how smelly we were, my immediate family stayed in the RV while Frank and Jean rented a motel room and offered the use of their shower. I'm actually not sure if any of the second cousins bathed that weekend. Everyone had too much fun to care.

Our RV seemed out of place in the charming neighborhood, a spread-out community of five-acre lots. Each home boasted meticulous landscaping, but Peggy's was unsurpassed: flower beds bordered by neatly trimmed shrubs, an ancient oak with a tire swing, meandering mulch paths lined by decorative stones, and grass as green as Ireland.

On the far edge of the property, a homely cinder brick blockhouse hid behind a thick hedge of mountain laurel and pine trees. Peggy thought that would be a good place for the RV.

"Plenty of shade," she said. And out of sight.

The cousins used it as a fort where they ate junk food and played cards, video games, and even board games like Parcheesi, Life, and Monopoly. They couldn't really trash the RV; it was already trashed.

Me, I explored the blockhouse, which was filled with dust-covered paraphernalia: ancient farm tools, the quintessential collection of mouse-chewed *Life* and *National Geographic* magazines, moldy butter churns and washboards, dried-out work boots that served as a home for the aforementioned mice, overalls and flannels that should have been rags, a kerosene lantern with broken glass, and other junk collected over several lifetimes.

My favorite item wasn't junk, though. It was an intricately tooled, Western saddle that any rider would be proud of. Half-kiddingly, I told Uncle Jimmy, Aunt Peggy's husband, "There's an old saddle in there, covered with dust. I'd be glad to take it off your hands."

Jimmy was a crusty, no-nonsense country boy. He just stared at me.

A little nervous now, I joked, "If you can't find it when we leave, don't go calling me."

I'd gone too far. His weathered forehead furrowed and his eyes scrunched into harsh slits. "If that saddle goes missing, I'm takin' it out o' yer hide, partner." Partner is what he called folks he didn't know and wasn't sure he liked. I decided to lie low for a while.

Uncle Jimmy and his older brother, a big game hunter in Africa, were raised on a large cotton plantation. Both were eccentrics. Exotic knickknacks and taxidermy animals hung in every room of the ranch house, not just the blockhouse, making it a personal museum of natural history.

Jimmy, an avid reader, was fixated on things Western. I settled into the family room's leather chair flanked by a dark-paneled wall lined with shelves of dusty, well-worn Westerns: Zane Grey, Louis L'Amour, Teddy Roosevelt, Larry McMurtry, etc., along with horns, antlers, taxidermy fish, and beavers. Above, a rustic plaque displayed different strands of twisted wire subtitled, *A History of the Barbed Wire That Fenced the West.*

While scanning his extensive collection, I finished a ham and cheese sandwich, the reunion's standard fare. When I absentmindedly tossed my mustard-stained napkin into a trashcan, I noticed toes on the wastebasket—big, gray wrinkly ones. I looked closer and saw that it was a hollowed-out foot from a bull elephant Jimmy's brother had killed during a 1920s African game hunt. Teddy Roosevelt would've been proud; there was one in his *Sagamore Hill* library.

The soft drinks ran right through me. After chucking my soda can into the elephant's foot, I headed for the bathroom, where open shelves above the toilet held some of the oddest gewgaws imaginable. One was especially notable: a sealed Mason jar filled with a yellowish liquid and a couple of wrinkled globs that looked almost like flesh. *I wonder what that is.*

I found Aunt Peggy's peculiar husband in the kitchen. *Maybe I can redeem myself after my saddle comments.* "Say ... Uncle Jim. That's quite a collection of books you've got."

"Humph, folks call me Jimmy."

"Okay, Jimmy it is." *One more chance.* "So, what's in that jar over the toilet?"

"My brother was roping a steer and got his thumb and forefinger twisted up in the rope. Ripped the damn things clean off. He thought it'd be nice to save 'em."

"That's incredible," I said.

"Like the saddle, it stays put—*partner.*"

Like I would want to abscond with such a horror.

Although a tough nut to crack, Jimmy was actually a nice guy—we got along fine once I realized he was more bark than bite. When we talked about horses and hillbillies, I mostly asked questions and seldom interjected. He liked that.

The town was quaint—the Mountain View Town Square was anchored by the courthouse, sheriff's office, and a two-cell jail. The other three sides were lined with ma & pa shops that sold everything from iron works to dry goods, an old-fashioned ice cream parlor, and a music store full of banjoes, dulcimers, and fiddles (no clarinets or French horns). Clothing stores sold jeans, flannels, boots, straw hats, and sundresses. Leather goods were for livestock—no tight chinos.

Throughout the day and into the evening, erstwhile musicians congregated in small groups on park benches, storefront porches, and alleyways. Three or four folks might comprise the impromptu sessions until a friend would saunter up with a guitar and start playing in the middle of a song. At that point, someone might quietly leave. The number of players was always fluid, as was the type of instrument. Most songs were wailed with a twang; some were good and some weren't. Clacking spoons and Jew's harps were common.

On Saturday night, the courthouse stage was put to more formal use, although random folk climbed up to barn-dance while a featured group played. Flatfooting was a favorite, and youngsters were especially fun to watch.

Local folks brought lawn chairs, stools, and blankets along with picnic baskets and coolers. Kids chased fireflies while teenagers smooched in the shadows. Alcohol was illegal, but moonshine-filled Mason jars made the rounds. The stone wall that edged the courthouse lawn was lined with tourists who didn't know enough to bring their own chairs.

Night after night was a veritable shindig.

Three days later, the reunion drew to a close and it was time to shake the RV loose. There were hugs and tears all around as we clambered aboard the rickety wreck, which now smelled more of adolescent sweat than mold and sewage. The engine groaned and with a clatter sprang to life. I half-expected it wouldn't start.

Kate wore her emotions on her sleeve, crying freely. At that, Peggy took her aside.

"Darling. Wipe those tears. We meet every three years. If we did it sooner, or if we lived near one another, we probably wouldn't be able to stand each other."

Kate gained her composure, and Peggy roared with laughter.

As we pulled away, Peggy smiled and waved good-bye. Jimmy nodded once and shuffled back to the house. In the passenger seat, Jean sat stone-faced—a stoic country girl. But I could tell she was sad about leaving her siblings who were scattered throughout the nation, as far away as Hawaii. In the rearview mirror, the homestead slowly grew smaller, then disappeared.

It was the last time we saw Uncle Jimmy. He died shortly after.

That Christmas, I sent each family a copy of a home movie I'd made of the reunion. It was the last audio-visual record of Jimmy. Peggy couldn't bring herself to watch it for a year.

CHAPTER TWELVE

Homeward Bound

W atch it! You're gonna hit that signpost," Frank said.
"Road's narrow, Frank. Ya want me to hit someone
head-on?"

Frank kept egging me. To keep calm, I suggested, "Why
don't you just relax and take a nap?"

"Not with you driving," he muttered.

"Not again, you two," Kate said, exasperated. "We've got a
long way to go."

After leaving Mountain View, Frank and I started to pick
up right where we left off, even though we both had had a
good time. To add to our angst, the brakes squeaked every
time I hit them. Frank glared as if I had done something
wrong while Jean sat at the kitchen table, staring out the
window as the town gave way to countryside. I decided right
then not to make any more waves.

Things between Frank and me quieted down once we hit
the interstate in Little Rock where our RV floated on its
spongy shocks. Clouds slowly gathered overhead, darkening
the morning sky.

"Let's stop at that KOA outside Nashville," Kate suggested. "We know where it is."

"Okay, but let's hope they don't remember we were the ones who junked the screen door," I said with a grin.

"Good point. But you're the one who left it." Frank couldn't help himself.

"Dad!"

"Just making fun, honey."

"Well, don't." Kate leaned into her mom.

For lunch, I successfully negotiated a Sonic fast-food drive-through. A light rain briefly sprinkled our campsite that night, but we weren't eating breakfast there anyway. Without refrigeration in the RV there was no point, and we knew where to find Denny's.

More black clouds rolled in as we wolfed down pancakes and omelets at the diner while the rain became steady. After we raced back to the RV, Frank looked for the windshield wiper button but couldn't find it. Rain had yet to be an issue, and I forgot where I'd discovered it while looking for the headlights.

"Let me look, Frank."

"Okay. This knob should be the one."

"You're right. There's a little picture of wipers on it."

"But nothing's happening." Frank sounded puzzled.

"I'll look under the hood." I'd always worked on my own cars, and Frank didn't want to stand out in the rain. We agreed to take a united stand against the evil RV.

"Here, take my umbrella." Kate always had one handy.

"I'm not gonna melt." I always refused.

"Suit yourself."

So in the diner parking lot, I got soaked while staring under the hood. I couldn't find anything wrong, but when I fiddled with the blades, they suddenly came to life, then ... stopped. I pulled one toward me and the other moved in tandem, then both automatically wiped across the windshield before stopping again. I figured out that if they were pulled to the passenger side, they magically went back. Like everything else in the RV, they about half worked.

"Hey, Frank. Let's tie a string around the one," I suggested. "I'll sit here and yank on it."

"Whatever works."

The kids searched every crack and cranny for a string or rope but came up empty-handed. The manager at Denny's claimed there was none to be had, or he didn't want to part with it.

Kate finally found an extension cord under the bed. "Will this work?"

"I guess." I wasn't sure why we had the electric cord, but I tied it to a wiper blade and, although not very pretty, it worked. Drenched to the bone, I climbed back inside.

"I told you to use the umbrella," Kate said smugly.

I shrugged and removed my shirt and shoes, and Jean volunteered to ride shotgun with her arm out the window while I dried out. She faithfully gave the extension cord rhythmic pulls while Frank sat high and dry in the captain's chair. We hit the highway with guarded confidence in our windshield wipers.

By the time we reached east Tennessee, it seemed we'd need a bailing bucket. Not only did rain blow in through the open window, but the roof leaked ... in a couple of places. The carpet became soaked yet again, while some excess water drained through the rusted floorboard.

As we passed by Bristol's famous speedway just off I-81, the Memorial Day traffic became horrendous, slowing to a crawl, then stop and go. The brakes complained ever louder until the traffic completely stopped, more than the typical holiday traffic jam. I became concerned about getting the kids back to school on time.

As we sat in the I-81 parking lot, our engine made a loud clatter, violently shimmied, and conked out. The starter turned over, but the thing wouldn't fire up.

"Did you kill it, Frank?" I forgot about keeping things upbeat.

"I didn't do anything. It just won't go. Why don't you see if that extension cord will help?" Frank said sarcastically. I took a second look under the hood, but it was a waste of time. I got soaked to the skin, again.

"Should've used the umbrella," Kate admonished.

"I'm telling you, I don't melt," I said, shivering.

"Stop acting like two-year-olds." Usually even-keeled, Jean was getting testy. "I'm pretty wet myself from yanking this stupid cord all day." For some reason, she continued to pull it even after we'd stopped, proving the battery worked fine.

The fast lane began to inch forward in fits and starts. While we sat stalled in the middle lane, a Virginia State Trooper drove up the shoulder and hopped out of his cruiser. He walked straight toward us, rain pouring off his plastic-covered, wide-brimmed hat, accentuating his foul mood. Frank rolled down his window and grinned. "Good afternoon, officer. What seems to be the problem?"

His rain gear drenched, the cop stared aggressively at my father-in-law before his attention was drawn to the windshield wipers, which Jean had continued to faithfully manipulate. "What the hell's that?" he pointed.

"Funny you should ask. We were getting ready to leave Nashville when it started to rain. We'd just had breakfast at Denny's and I tried to find the wiper button ..."

"Look, Mister. You've got to move this rig off the road. This traffic jam is backed up for miles, and you're making things worse. A semi jackknifed and it's blocking the whole road, so you'll have to move this vehicle out of the way."

"Now that's a problem, officer. You see, the damn thing

just stopped—dead. It won't go. But the electric works. We've got wipers—sort of." Frank loved to mess with people's heads.

I thought, *Not now! Not with a state trooper.*

"I'll call for a tow truck," he said with a growl. "Might be awhile, though."

"Thanks, officer, and you have a nice day."

The cop glared before marching away.

"Damn, Frank. Pushing it a little, don't you think? He might never call for help."

"Yeah, he will. He wants us out of the way."

Three miserable hours later—when the kids were more than antsy—the tow truck finally made it through the traffic. The burly driver, sporting a handlebar mustache and unshaven face, looked about as happy as the cop had as he took a while maneuvering around cars and into position. He didn't want to work in this holiday mess any more than the next guy. When he climbed out of the truck, his sleeveless shirt became wetter than a mop while he weaved toward Frank's window.

"Do you want us to get out?" Frank cheerfully asked as Kate tightly gripped her umbrella.

"Nah, ya'll stay put." Rain poured off the bill of his baseball cap. "I'll hook her up and git ya back to the station."

The kids were excited that they could stay inside while the RV was towed. Everyone gathered around the windshield to watch him work.

He let out a length of chain from the towing crane and bent low to attach it. With no belt to hold his pants up, he might've been a plumber in a previous life. Rivulets trickled into places that no rain should have to go. Without a word he hopped back into his truck and started the winch. The RV began to lift as Russell and Tara cheered. We rose ever higher until the front wheels lifted far off the ground. It felt like an amusement park ride, until ...

Riiiiip!

The RV suddenly dropped in a free-fall and hit the pavement with a resounding crash. Kate and I knocked heads while the kids tumbled onto the soggy floor.

"What the hell just happened?" Frank exclaimed.

"Look!" Jean pointed. Our bumper dangled on the tow truck's chain, the strong wind periodically slamming it into our hood. The driver hadn't attached the hook to the frame and the bumper pulled loose.

Jean, who never said anything bad about anyone, said, "What an idiot." Disgusted with the whole ordeal, she had reached the end of her rope—or extension cord.

Without a word of explanation, the driver threw the corroded bumper into the back of his truck and attached the hook to the frame. Skirting around traffic on the shoulder, we passed the semi that had jackknifed. It had been transporting eggs, and thousands were scattered and broken. Wytheville County would smell to high heaven once the sun began to beat down.

We soon pulled into a gas station. The RV wouldn't fit into a bay, so the mechanic on duty waited for the storm to pass before checking the engine. "Needs a new fuel pump," he announced.

"That shouldn't take long," I said, trying to sound upbeat. "We should be on our way in a couple hours.

"Nope," he said matter-of-factly. "Today's a holiday. Supply house don't open 'til tomorrow."

The kids were happy about missing an extra day of school, but Jean, agitated, paced the wet parking lot. "So where're we supposed to stay?"

"Best thing I can think of ma'am is your RV."

"Here? In a gas station?"

"Yep." He smiled politely. "If ya need food, there's a quickie mart inside."

"Oh, my God," Jean said. "I can't believe this is really happening." She was ready for her own bed, her own shower, and real food. We all were, except Tara and Russell. I gave them money for snacks and they returned with Twinkies, Cokes, and potato chips—they couldn't have been happier.

We arranged the beds for one more night; no one would be sleeping outside at the gas station. With no amenities in the RV, every time we wanted to use the bathroom we had to ask the attendant for the key.

Jean, Frank, Kate, and I sat inside the RV and stared at nothing in particular. "I know it's Memorial Day, but this place sure seems busy," Frank commented, breaking the silence.

"Yeah, listen," Kate echoed.

Full service gas stations once had those black compression hoses that trailed across the asphalt and rang a bell to alert the attendant whenever a vehicle rolled in. They're not around anymore, but this station still had one, and it was ringing every few seconds.

Kate pulled back the frayed curtain on the side door window and said, "Oh no!"

Crouching between two pumps on the center island, Tara and Russell shouted in unison, "One, two, three—now!" In tandem, they jumped onto the hose, activating the bell. Exhausted, I stepped outside and shouted, "That's enough!" Sugar-charged, they giggled and went into the store for more junk food.

Darkness fell as the glare from mercury vapor lamps filtered through the thin curtains of our stranded motel-on-wheels. Frank riffled through the cluttered storage closet, desperately in search of something. "Here it is." He held up a lei that Jean's brother from Hawaii had brought for each of us. An assortment of seven miniature liquor bottles hung from them.

Frank expected alcoholic relief; instead, all the bottles were empty. He found a second lei only to discover that it was also devoid of any liquid comfort. A third was the same.

"What the hell happened to all the booze?"

Clueless, Kate and I looked at each other. "I didn't drink any," I said a little guiltily.

Jean was discreetly propped up in the driver's seat with her lips pursed in a slight grin; a decided glow radiated from her checks. She seldom drank, but circumstances demanded extreme measures. Throughout the rainy afternoon, she'd polished off all the island treats without anyone noticing.

"I'm tired, think I'll go to bed." Jean swayed down the narrow passageway and dropped into the double bed. Who knew she snored?

I volunteered to sleep in the narrow space above the cab and gave Tara my spot on the table/bed with Kate. Russell curled up in the captain's chair.

Having miscounted my underwear before the trip, and with our vacation extended by the breakdown, my last pair was on its third day. I couldn't stand the idea of wearing them all night, so I discreetly took them off after climbing into my bedroll. *I'll throw them away when we get home*, I thought.

There were numerous big rigs parked off to the side of the gas station. At five in the morning, the drivers fired them up—simultaneously—each intent on gunning his more than the next guy. The noise was deafening.

At the unexpected roar of a dozen powerful diesels, I sat up and slammed my head on the roof. "Ouch! Damn it. Who arranged for the wake-up call?" I growled before tossing my underwear at the passenger seat below me. I didn't think anyone else was up.

I was wrong. Kate's Mom was sitting there, nursing a hangover. While watching the glow of dawn, my three-day-old skivvies landed square on her face. She screamed, ran from the cab, and dashed into the quickie mart for the key to the public commode. She spent a long time washing up before returning.

I was forever living it down.

⌾

Later that morning, while eating a breakfast of chips and Mountain Dew, I waited outside for the fuel pump, which was installed in short order. The day was sunny while we rode uneventfully up I-81. At first no one talked much; the lack of booze for Frank and the aerial attack of my dirty underwear probably contributed to the silence. After being up half the night, Tara and Russell slept.

As we got closer to home, and without anyone saying anything, Kate started to quietly chuckle. I looked at her and grinned.

Frank then smiled and said, "It's been one hell of a ride."

At that, all of us started to reminisce and belly laugh. We had survived a trek in what was possibly the most broken-down RV in the country, but the last leg from Charlottesville to the Potomac River was filled with merriment. Even the kids woke up and joined in the fun.

I didn't anticipate any more RV trips in the near future.

CHAPTER THIRTEEN

Culture Shock /
Highway Shock

I often heard the following at parties when people found out I was a dentist:

"I don't mind it when the pretty nurse cleans my teeth, but I hate the dentist."

"Mine said I have a cavity, but it doesn't hurt. I think he just wants the money."

"After the last guy drilled a tooth, I needed a root canal."

So it goes when the host announces, "Hey, look. Dr. Pain is here."

Folks in the waiting room didn't usually talk that way; they were too nervous. Instead, they tended to silently fidget or work their knees like jackhammers. Waiting room furniture was built super-sturdy to take the abuse.

Trish, my new assistant, had come highly recommended by her old boss. Like Natalia, she was of the Gucci persuasion. Trish had taken a few years off to have a baby and was a little rusty when I hired her, but she soon got back into the groove.

Trish was Lebanese and spoke fluent Spanish; however, I

found her English hard to understand. Kate and I therefore agreed that she should never answer the phone. At her interview, I asked Trish if pronunciation was a problem in her last office.

"No problem. Bozz be Lebanese and clients too. Accent, think I got?"

She talks like Yoda. "It's not a problem, Trish, but call them patients."

Determined, her diction quickly improved, although she still stumbled over my Southern colloquialisms when trying to imitate them. Y'all became yah and sweetie morphed into sweaty. It's tough to translate hominy grits and succotash; Chitlins and catawampus were the ultimate challenges.

One year, Trish was giving her four-year-old daughter a birthday party and invited Kate and me. I tried to excuse us from a party for a kid we didn't really know by offering a card and small present she could give to her.

Trish feigned offense. "No like Soya?"

Reluctantly, we agreed to go, "but only for a short time." I anticipated just a few relatives gathered at the grandmother's small apartment, telling Kate, "How many Lebanese can there be in Gaithersburg?"

Apparently a lot.

We parked and heard loud music. Hordes of swarthy folks headed toward the apartment building it was coming from.

I looked at Kate. "I think that's the place."

We squeezed through a dense throng of revelers smoking on the stairwell and were greeted by a pleasant middle-aged lady.

"You Trish's bozz-man?"

Our pale skin probably gave us away.

"Cum, mit zon. He docteur." Trish's brother seemed nice enough, but no one ever mentioned his name, just that he was a doctor.

Grandma proudly showed us her buffet. I placed a few exotic delicacies on my paper plate while Kate, a picky eater, grabbed some olives and a piece of hard bread. I sat on the only unoccupied chair, and Kate crossed her legs on the floor beside me. After a serious accident (see Chapter Nineteen), that was the only way she could comfortably sit for any length of time. "The Docteur" nodded his approval of her subservience. Unbeknownst to him, Kate was anything but.

At eye level, we couldn't see much through the crowd of bellies and butts, but I did glimpse a flicker when the candles were lit on the cake. Everyone sang a Lebanese Happy Birthday, followed by the familiar English version. Kate and I joined in the latter.

At that point, a brigade of sugar-charged kids wildly weaved through the forest of legs, settling down only when Soya began to unwrap her extravagant presents. *I must be paying Trish too much*, I thought. Afterward, the children were banished to the back rooms.

Booze flowed freely from a full-service bar jury-rigged on a card table, and the crowd magically cleared to make a dance floor in the living room where the adults took center stage. They began to pulsate to tinny, rhythmic music that was cranked way too high. Men strutted around like peacocks while women erotically shimmied their strapless tops. It quickly no longer resembled any toddler's birthday party I'd ever been to.

"Kate," I whispered. "Now's a good time to leave."

I helped her up and looked around for Trish, whom we hadn't seen much of. She was getting a refill at the bar when I found her.

"We've got to be going now, Trish. It's been fun and … interesting."

"No! Can't go. Party just starting."

Apparently, we were on the verge of committing a cultural faux pas by leaving. Although I had to work early the next morning, as did Trish, we agreed to stay a little longer. Kate and I tried to sneak out later, when Trish was out of sight, but grandma blocked the door while balancing two plates of Lebanese delicacies for us.

"Thanks," I muttered while juggling my overloaded plate through the intoxicated crowd. *I thought Arabs couldn't drink?*

I was wrong.

Trish rolled into work a bit later than usual the next morning as a couple of anxious folks were already fidgeting in the waiting room. After a second cup of coffee, she opened the door and announced in an accent harsher than usual, "Doog, das dicteur to see yu now." All Doug heard was *Doog* and *now.* He slowly stood and put the crumpled *People* magazine, which he wasn't really reading, back into the rack. When he missed the slot and it splayed onto the floor, he retrieved it with a shaky hand while sporting a silly grin.

A dental appointment could be a bit nerve-wracking, like any doctor's visit. Even pet owners might get a little antsy when taking Fluffy to the vet; there were only those cavalier few who exhibited no trepidation whatsoever.

Charlene, a high school classmate of Kate's, was one of the latter. A thick-skinned jock, Charlene could've been mistaken for a Soviet-bloc Olympian on steroids. But she hadn't been to a dentist since moving out of her parents' house. No longer footing her bills, her dad's loving advice was similar to my dad's: "Get a job, ya bum—and one with decent insurance."

After a few menial jobs, she landed a good one. When her insurance kicked in, Charlene called Kate at home. "That bozo you work for any good?"

"Well, I trust him." Then, "You do know that I'm married to that bozo?"

"Yeah, whatever. How 'bout a checkup tomorrow morning?"

"I don't think there are any openings tomorrow, Charlene. Why don't you call the office in the morning? Irene will take care of you."

"Okay, but I thought you might slip me in, being my friend and all."

"You'll see the hygienist first," Kate said to gently placate her.

A couple weeks later, Tania cleaned Charlene's teeth and noticed quite a few cavities.

"If Dr. Carroll doesn't get to these soon, you might need root canals or even lose a few teeth." Tania was insistent, but as always, in a pleasant way.

Charlene wasn't fazed. "Just tell him to do what he's gotta do," she loudly declared.

Several appointments were needed to finish her work, but over the course of treatment, Charlene was never late and always relaxed. I could do almost anything on her and all she did was snooze. What's more, nothing developed into a root canal.

Six months later, she scheduled a regular checkup. This time, she was a half hour late. I glanced at the clock. *That's not like Charlene.* Washington was notorious for its traffic jams, so I thought maybe she got caught up in one. Kate thought it unlikely that she forgot; Charlene was very responsible. Nevertheless, Irene decided to call her work.

"She left about forty-five minutes ago," they told Irene. More than enough time, even in heavy traffic.

"She late. Ver be she? Need get here." Trish wasn't at all concerned.

Conversely, Irene seemed worried. "Forty-five minutes is a long time to be stuck in traffic."

"If she shows up soon, I can still treat her." Tania was always willing to bend over backwards for her patients. "I hope she's okay."

"Still late," said Trish, annoyed.

Suddenly, the waiting room door opened with a loud crash. The doorstop went flying as Charlene blew in, wild-eyed. Without pausing at the reception window, she bulled straight to the treatment area. She was rather pale, in contrast to the nice summer tan she usually sported. Sweat poured down her face, seemingly unrelated to the July heat or her upcoming cleaning. She paced the back hallway while her body shook uncontrollably.

Charlene gathered a modicum of composure and babbled incoherently. "Big flatbed ... traffic jam ... red light ... holy s***!"

Kate grabbed her arm. "Slow down, Char. What happened?"

"Metal pole ... flag ...." Her rambling was making no sense.

Kate coaxed her into my private office and offered her a seat. "Calm down, Charlene. Do you want something to drink? Just tell me what happened."

Unable to answer, Charlene couldn't sit still. She was like a jack-in-the-box, popping up as soon as her butt hit the seat, then pacing circles around the office.

Her voice shook. "Ca ... can't believe I'm alive! Kate, I could've been killed ... or worse!"

Worse?

The story slowly unfolded. She'd left work early to get gas. After waiting in line forever for a discount, she was now running late. The flow of bumper-to-bumper cars on Rockville Pike made it almost impossible for her to pull out. Finally, a Good Samaritan gave her a break.

Whenever I was in a hurry, I seemed to hit every red light and therefore tended to floor it between signals. It never did any good, but that's also what Charlene did.

A sizable flatbed had stopped at the next signal when she gunned it, and Charlene gauged her breaking distance to its rear bumper. She was still moving fast when there was a horrendous crash. Safety glass splattered onto the front seat as her little car jolted to a stop. She felt a bruise across her chest from the seatbelt (airbags weren't standard then).

In a confused whirl, her brain couldn't account for her broken windshield. She practically stood on the brake pedal while she tried to figure it out. As her heart wildly raced, she turned to see a huge steel 'I' beam beside her. It had come within inches of her head and stopped over the back seat, still with the requisite red flag tied to it. In a hurry, Charlene hadn't noticed its futile waving in the slight breeze of this sultry summer day. It now dangled limp. Amazingly, the only damage to the car was the windshield.

Charlene was fine, but I'll bet nightmares became a problem.

"Why don't we reschedule your hygiene appointment, Char?" I offered.

She declined, despite her near-death experience. "I'm here now. Let's just do it." Believe it or not, she calmed down and almost fell asleep while Tania cleaned her teeth. That's what I called relaxed.

"Good, she late, no more." Trish shook her head. "Get less cavities."

Charlene was never again late for an appointment. After she moved from the area, I wondered if she bought a Hummer to replace the little compact.

CHAPTER FOURTEEN

———————

An Interlude on "The Ridge"

Nealy Ridge was a meandering knife-edged mountain hidden in Virginia's southwest corner between West Virginia, Kentucky, and nowhere. It nestled comfortably amongst likeminded Appalachian peaks where ancient rivers and streams wound aimlessly through steep canyons. Birds soared on updrafts in search of carrion; the sky was cobalt blue, and the region remained beautiful into the twenty-first century.

In the 1950s, a rutted, one-lane dirt road, unmarked by so much as a homemade sign and looking more like a neglected farm lane, coursed along the overhanging cliffs and around hairpin switchbacks. Chain gangs scattered gravel on those stretches likely to be washed away by heavy rains. As a result, driving up that road could be quite scary. At the top of The Ridge, a rocky, semi-flat patch of ground witnessed the birth of my mother, her sister, and their two brothers.

In the hot summer of 1999, several of my aunts, uncles, cousins, second cousins, and those twice removed—whatever that means—met at a park near the Bristol Speedway. While sweltering in the thick steamy air, we gnawed on chicken wings and spat watermelon seeds, all the while swatting at the ever-present flies and yellow jackets.

Uncle BJ dominated the conversation, jawing about old times up on The Ridge. I was familiar with many stories, but not all. When he paused to take a long draw on his cigarette, I snuck an advantage.

"I heard Dickenson County just got its first traffic light."

When I was a kid, the main intersection in Clintwood had a three-way stop. The steep mountain behind the county courthouse precluded a fourth road. A dry goods store sat on one corner while a small Ford dealership spread up the hill from the south side. Boasting only made-in-the-USA vehicles, mostly pickups, it overlooked the tiny town of modest, ramshackle homes.

BJ blew a smoke ring, cleared his throat, and leaned forward. His weathered visage became deadly serious as his piercing eyes stared over the top of his half-lens spectacles like a Southern judge. *Uh Oh.* Nervous that I'd broached a sore subject, I stared back, afraid to blink or break eye contact, although I desperately wanted to.

Breaking into a wide toothy grin, BJ held up a couple of arthritic fingers and proudly exclaimed, "We got two!"

I started to breathe again. In the 1950s there were no stoplights ... or streetlights—just the occasional porch light.

Although the town boasted a small water tower, outlying Dickenson County was a land of draw-wells, outhouses, mule-drawn ploughs, horse-drawn wagons, wood stoves, party lines and, of special interest to kids, one-room school houses. The three Rs—readin', 'ritin', and 'rithmetic—were taught to all grades under a single tin roof. Aunt Bessie, BJ's wife and Grandma's youngest sister of nine siblings, all girls, was the schoolmarm on The Ridge when I was growing up.

Although obsolete today, telephone party lines were

common. Three or four houses would have different numbers but share the phone line, so the only phone in each house would ring with a distinct pattern: two shorts and a long, two longs and a short, etc.

One could answer the phone in any of the houses sharing the same line, and Mom and Aunt Aida often eavesdropped on neighbors by quietly lifting the receiver. Because Grandma strongly disapproved of such unseemly behavior, they were careful not to get caught. If a neighbor tied up the line too long, my staid grandmother would pick up her phone. "Lulu, are ye gonna blabber all blessed day?" Grandma was no-nonsense.

As subsistence farmers, my grandparents grew most everything they ate and made most of their clothes. Grandpa earned some money by felling trees with the help of a neighbor and a crosscut saw. The limbed logs were taken down the mountain by horse-drawn wagon and sold to a lumber mill, the deal sealed with a handshake. It was hard work.

With this hard-earned cash, Grandma purchased sugar, flour, and bolts of cloth in Clintwood where Grandpa also bought coarse overalls and boots. The store was a full day's trip down and back up the mountain, so folks seldom went off The Ridge.

Like their far-flung neighbors, they raised chickens, beef cattle, and dairy cows. Pigs were butchered only on special occasions. A nearby neighbor bred workhorses, which he sold at the county fair.

More than once, while shuffling bleary-eyed to the outhouse at morning milking time, I strayed too close to the business end of a cow. Grandpa's eyes would twinkle while a glow lit up his wizened face. He'd firmly grasp a swollen teat and send a warm stream my way. Quickly looking back to the bag, he'd affect an attitude of innocence. In the heat of summer, I smelled like sour milk the rest of the day.

Because refrigeration was unknown on The Ridge, milk was always fresh and warm with a thick, hoary head; hand-churned butter was the only way to store it. As a child, my mother hated churning and all but refused to make butter during our working summers. Aunt Aida, her sister, usually got stuck with that chore.

One year, Grandpa enlarged a small cave in the north face of a knoll about fifty yards from his farmhouse. For shelving, he laid rough-hewn boards across rock outcroppings and sealed the entrance with a heavy wooden door. Only four or five feet high inside, the cave remained fairly cool in summertime. Along with butter and vegetables, Grandma stored canned goods, boiled and sealed in Mason jars. That's how I first learned the principle of autoclaving instruments.

Across the road from the farmhouse, the flattest patch of ground for a garden was a two-acre clearing that was still steep. Grandpa trudged behind his hardy mule to plow that sad, rocky field. With the reins loosely wrapped around his sun-reddened neck, he'd firmly grasp the plow's wooden handles with his strong, calloused hands. "Ye haw, ge' on up thar' ole gal," he'd yell as it struggled to cut a furrow in the unyielding ground. I sometimes imagined Grandpa and mule, conjoined by the heavy plow-beam, toppling sideways and rolling forever down the hill. But it never happened.

That modest plot provided the family with vegetables, fresh or vacuum-sealed, for the entire year. It was a tough life. But I loved my summers down home. It all started when Mom left The Ridge for a better life in Washington DC, where she met my father, a city-bred dandy ...

CHAPTER FIFTEEN

Country Meets City

I n the pitch-black of an Appalachian night, a wet, slightly slumped silhouette stood in the darkened doorway of Grandpa's farmhouse. Dad had ventured outside to "water the flowers" but came back looking like something had watered him; it was puddling around his feet.

In the high-back spindle chair at the head of Grandma's dimly lit kitchen table, Uncle Joel blew thick smoke rings from a hand-rolled cigarette. He clutched the winning poker hand and a Mason jar. Regal, like a Scottish earl, he looked my father up and down and gulped a swig of moonshine. As rocket-fuel dribbled from one corner of his mouth, he grinned. "What the hell happened to you, Harry?"

"Nuthin'," my future dad said with a huff. Joel offered him another belt, but Harry had had enough for one night, and for the weekend. A beer man, he wasn't used to white lightning.

Grandpa's porch was much closer than the outhouse, but it lacked railings. "Extravagant nonsense," according to Grandpa. Dad had gone to the far end where the Appalachian hillside sloped sharply away and a wooden barrel stored rainwater for washing clothes, dishes, and people. The 55-gallon hoop and stave drum lacked a lid.

In his compromised state, and in the total darkness of a high mountain night, Harry took one wobbly step too many. "What the ...!"

Family lore was never quite clear on how he managed to wiggle out, but in the cool plunge he sobered up in a jiffy. The modest glow from the kitchen bulb, which hung by a frayed electric cord, revealed several contusions and minor cuts on his arms and legs. Unlike men in Dickenson County, Harry wore shorts; the checkered Bermudas were torn along with his Hawaiian shirt. His waterlogged wingtips were all but ruined.

Dad had left his cards face-down on the table, which was a little naïve for an experienced poker player. He was pretty drunk, and Joel's hillbilly cronies had no scruples about taking advantage of the flatlander.

One scrawny good ole boy with a high-pitched voice smiled too much. He tried to peek at Harry's cards, but Joel stopped him. Another sat stone-still and grunted while fiddling with his poker chips, a pile that grew as Dad's diminished. Another beefy, ruddy man seemed downright scary.

With his kindly visage, Uncle BJ was the successful, clean-cut family man at the table. He kept his money in a billfold rather than wadded and stuffed in dirty overalls.

"Harry, you're gonna lose yer shirt to them boys." Mom, her grammar reverting to hillbilly, saw things all too clearly. But Harry kept right on playing, drinking, and losing until he staggered outside to escape her scathing glare and tend to business. Now, he was finished with cards and booze for the night. Mom sported a not-so-subtle victory smirk. He was about out of cash anyway while the hillbillies were that much richer, and they didn't extend credit to a grown man in short pants.

∽

My father, born in 1899, was raised in urban southeast DC. Mom was reared in the backwoods of southwestern Virginia, having entered the world in 1921. Yet these two, so far apart in age and backgrounds, fell in love, married, and raised two boys.

I never spent time shooting the breeze with Dad, simply because he was so old. But after I had my own kids, I wanted to know more about him. Tara, his first grandchild, was the girl he'd always wanted after raising four boys, two of whom were my half-brothers. With baby Russell perched on one knee and Tara sitting on the arm of his easy chair, Dad freely related the adventures and misadventures of his colorful life.

Harry loved racehorses. The excitement of the track fed his gambling instinct, along with the quintessential poker game. Immediately following WWI, long before Castro strangled Cuba in his heartless grip, Dad shipped a couple of thoroughbreds to Havana. He and his jockey knew they'd make a killing there.

After a discouraging month, the money ran out and Dad was forced to sell; he borrowed fifty dollars from his jockey for passage back to Miami in ship's steerage. He'd attacked destiny head-on and lost. Back in the States, he vowed to never again own a racehorse, although he continued betting at the track. Not only was gambling in his blood, but he loved those spirited animals, imparting that same feeling to me and Lee, my brother. Early evidence is shown in a grainy black-and-white of me on horseback when I was about a year old—Dad's smiling and holding the reins … and me.

In the late twenties, during Prohibition, Harry owned a busy diner on Capitol Hill that catered to politicians, but short-order lunches weren't the big money maker. For that, Dad kept a jug of hard liquor under the counter. Pols would order a sandwich and scope out the clientele to see if any looked suspicious. "I'll take a cup of your *special* coffee, Harry," they'd say.

The jug sat on a hinged shelf above a trough of lye. If a suspected US Treasury agent wandered in, Harry could simply pull a cord to dump the booze, rendering it unfit for human consumption and no longer illegal. "I never dumped one jug," Dad said with a smile. Small-time purveyors were mostly left alone, especially those who catered to Congress. It was great tax-free money.

The Twenty-First Amendment, repealing the Eighteenth, almost destroyed his livelihood. He turned from running numbers for the local mob as a youngster to booking numbers as an adult. He did live to see the Lotto: the government became the mob. Dad was ahead of his time.

His young wife's background couldn't have been more different. In the spring of '39, as misguided appeasement set the stage for WWII, the country girl left Nealy Ridge after graduating from the one-room schoolhouse. Bound for the nation's capital, she was set on making her fortune in the big city, as opportunities simply didn't exist for the large impoverished family she loved so much. Tearfully waving good-bye, she left her mountain home and hitched a ride to the Greyhound station in Clintwood, beyond which a world awaited.

Young and determined, Gaye arrived at the DC depot clad in the only brand-new dress and pair of shoes she'd ever owned, going-away presents from her pa. Her liquid assets comprised a small packet of crumpled-up bills and some loose change, which was modest even during the Depression. This small stake was carefully sheltered in a leather pouch strung around her neck.

"Keep this 'ere poke hid under yer clothes and don't never take it out in front of nobody," Grandpa said, mistrustful of the outside world.

Gaye had no ID on her, not even a driver's license. The

only thing she'd ever driven was a hay wagon hitched to a mule. Grandma kept all birth records in the family Bible but they were rarely needed—everyone on The Ridge knew who you were. Mom assumed things would be about the same in Washington, but she soon found out otherwise. Coming from tough Scots-Irish stock, however, survive she did.

She soon landed a job at Georgetown Jewelers. The proprietor, Frank, liked her friendly ways, while her accent gave the place an exotic flare—quaintness sometimes pays dividends.

Sometime before Mom arrived, Harry was featured on the cover of a national magazine as the Best-Dressed Man in Washington DC. Prominent in a black tux with shiny silk lapels, white cummerbund, top hat, ivory-topped cane, and patent leather spats, his photo was flanked by that of other major city dandies. He shopped at Frank's, the premier jewelry store of its time.

My mother, the unsophisticated mountain lass, was easily impressed with this man-of-the-world, infatuated by his big-city ways. Unlike Mom with her leather sack, Harry kept his folded greenbacks in a pewter clip, tucked into the front pocket of his stylish, pleated pants. Whenever he was riding high (which wasn't all the time), he proudly flaunted his money and could be generous to a fault.

Although considerably older than Gaye, Harry was still handsome—and charming. When asked to be his bride, she jumped at the chance. Their high Episcopal wedding was a bit "popish" for a Southern Baptist, but she adapted and became a life-long member of the Ancient Church. Only after they were married did the groom meet her family.

The bumpy two-and-a-half day's drive to the far edge of the earth was an eye-opener for Harry. As the newlyweds ventured south on the two-lane Valley Turnpike, they drove through every Podunk town, village, and hamlet along the Shenandoah River.

"I was checking the map at the Lexington Hotel last night," Dad announced. "Looks like we'll be there early."

Gaye just smiled, knowing that Clintwood seemed closer to Route 11 on a map than it really was. The turnoff was where the real adventure would begin.

As the potholed country road narrowed, Harry's shiny black Buick became quickly covered in a layer of dust, its whitewalls no longer white. His stylish pride and joy was well suited for paved city streets, but not for the washed-out macadam of Dickenson County, where it was out of place alongside the rusty, sawed-off trucks and horse-drawn wagons that moseyed along. Everyone gawked, including the mules.

Harry's tank of a car was too wide to easily negotiate the foothills, often veering into side ditches when approaching an oncoming vehicle. As they ventured deep into a narrow valley, the road became even less inviting. Harry's mood, not great since leaving the state road, didn't improve. But Gaye didn't notice, distracted by all the familiar landmarks. Excited, she pointed to a small break in the woods on the right and squealed, "There it is!"

His eyes strained. "There's what?"

"The road up to Ma's place."

Harry pulled off as far as he dared without slipping into the creek bed. He stopped and looked at the rutted dirt lane, little more than a cow path of roots and rocks. It became incredibly steep less than a hundred yards up. "You want me to go up that? It's not as wide as my car!"

"Yep, that's the only way." She shook with excitement while he anxiously eyeballed the cliffs. "Remember to blow yer horn on the curves," she said, "in case anyone's coming 'round the sharp bend."

This little tidbit did nothing to settle his nerves.

Dickenson County's treacherous, single-lane mountain roads were carved into the steep sides of towering mountains.

Although negotiating them was a simple fact of life for the locals, it was not so for Mr. Harry James. Whenever a vehicle approached, one car had to back into a shallow pocket that had been blasted out of the cliff. The rule was that whoever was the closest backed up to allow the other guy to pass. In all the years I traveled the mountain with Dad, he never once backed up, but instead stubbornly sat tight until the other fellow relinquished.

There were few autos on The Ridge, and most were rusty wrecks with smoke billowing from exhaust pipes that hung by coat hangers; a cracked window or two was common. The brakes, which were usually in good repair, could spell the difference between life and death.

Harry hesitated to climb heavenward, but his bride was watching. While his eyes darted through the tunnel of overhanging branches—his moist hands white-knuckled on the padded steering wheel—he reluctantly turned into the lane. As the Buick crept up the increasingly steep grade, sweat poured from his brow, blurring his sunglasses. Sticker bushes scraped the doors on the high side while the sheer drop-off edged ever closer.

Before the first hairpin turn, he made a command decision. "I'm not going up this damn mountain." That was probably a good call; for Harry, backing around one of those bends would've been nuts. The last time I went up, there was still no guardrail on a cliff that's no less sheer than it was eighty years ago.

The newlyweds spent the night in the venerable, yet spider-infested Black Coal Hotel in Clintwood, the only game around. Gaye lay awake all night, frustrated with her new hubby. In the morning, she marched up Main Street to BJ and Bessie's house, beside the Ford dealership.

"Morning, Uncle BJ. My new husband won't drive up The Ridge. Can you help?"

"Sure, honey. I'll drive ya'll up." BJ smiled as he grabbed his fedora from a hook. "So when did ya git back in town, little girl?"

"Yesterday. Spent the night in the Black Coal. Mama's probably wondering where I am."

At the hotel, Gaye introduced Harry to BJ, who grinned like the quintessential car salesman he was. He extended his big hand for a firm shake and gave Harry a hearty slap on the back. With a twinkle in his eye, BJ got right to the point. "Scared of the mountain, huh?"

"No. Well ... maybe a little. I'm just not used to it."

"Nice car. Your'n?" BJ strolled around, inspecting the Buick with a keen eye.

Dad smiled proudly but kept his guard up. "Sure is, bought and paid for."

"It's a beaut, wanna sell it? Give ya a good deal." Uncle BJ was a born horse trader, but so was Harry, and both loved poker. They became good friends.

Gaye smacked BJ's arm. "We just wanna git up ta Ma's place, sometime today if ya don' mind." Her hillbilly had gotten thicker.

BJ plopped into the driver's seat and turned the key. "Automatic starter—nice! And purrs like a kitten. If ya change your mind, I got a sturdy '36 Ford pickup that'll go up that mountain."

Harry sat in the back of his luxury sedan like a dejected schoolboy. He refused to gaze out the downhill window and stared straight ahead instead.

At each blind switchback, BJ laid on the horn and turned and looked at Dad. "Gotta make sure no one's comin' 'round the bend, Harry," he grinned.

"Please keep your eyes front," Dad countered.

When they neared Mom's old farmstead, BJ laid on the horn and hit the accelerator. He then slammed on the brakes and skidded to a dusty halt in Grandpa's scratch yard. Harry jumped out of his skin, positive they were going off the edge.

"Handles real nice Harvey. Let me know if ya change yer mind 'bout trading her."

"It's Harry."

Gaye glared at her uncle, who was yanking Dad's chain.

At the sound of the horn, Gaye's parents and a couple of neighbors came running outside to greet her and her new husband. Squeals of delight echoed throughout the hills.

"We were a little worried when you didn't arrive yesterday," Grandpa said, seldom expressing concern. "Maybe we should git one of them newfangled telephones," he suggested to Grandma. (They finally got one years later; I remember it being installed.)

A little shaky, Harry climbed out of the back seat and scraped his thigh on the door jamb. "Damn."

All those broad grins froze. Men didn't cuss in mixed company.

It was Southern summer hot, and Harry had dressed comfortably in his new plaid Bermuda shorts, all the rage in Washington. Stylish Mr. James wanted to impress the hick relatives—but didn't. His bright orange and white striped shirt that hung loosely over his belly was counterproductive, and except on movie posters at Clintwood's new drive-in, sunglasses were unknown—until now. He also wore sandals—only loose women wore toeless shoes, something young bucks kept their eyes peeled for.

I imagine Grandpa was thinking, *Why don't he jus' go barefoot? And where's his trousers?*

Grandma stared at his face. *Sumthing wrong with his eyes? Man's so white; looks sickly.*

After Dad's expletive, the down-home smiles soon returned. This was Gaye's husband, and as the folks looked him over, Harry was sure they were impressed. Grandpa, in his mud-encrusted clod-hoppers, overalls, and a torn cotton shirt, all topped off with a beat-up straw hat, grasped Harry's well-manicured hand in his strong, calloused one. Each gave the other a vigorous shake; both men appreciated a firm howdy.

Grandma presented in a plain sack dress and comfortable work shoes, with her hair pinned up in a loose bun. She nearly bowled Harry over when she threw her arms around his neck to plant a kiss on his cheek. "Welcome to the family," she said. Her prodigal daughter beamed. Harry was only a year younger than his new mother-in-law, but it didn't matter—older husbands weren't unusual in a region where many women died in childbirth.

Three sheds of rough-cut lumber defined the humble scratch yard, and pigs snorted within a rickety split-rail pen on the trail that led to the outhouse. From somewhere deep in the woods a cowbell warbled—the cow would wander back at milking time when her sack became full. Chickens pecked around the tires of the dusty black Buick as if to say that it was out of place.

Gaye was excited. "Come on in," she said while skipping toward the whitewashed, two-story farmhouse. Harry's large bull-head was sweeping from side to side, taking in the strange sights, when his half-naked foot plopped into a cow pie. Puzzled that a grown man would step without looking, Grandma took his arm and led him to a patch of wiry grass in the front yard where he could wipe it off. He never again wore sandals on the farm.

Although Gaye was embarrassed, Grandpa just grinned as the entourage backtracked to the side door. They seldom used the formal front entrance, which was reserved for pastoral visits. A little baffled by it all, Harry climbed the cockeyed steps up to the porch, the one from which he would igno-miniously topple during the poker game. Once indoors, everyone quickly made Mom's new husband, who was gen-uinely likeable, feel like family.

From the start, Uncle Joel often played good-natured tricks on Dad. My mountain forebears bantered with folks they liked and only tolerated people they didn't. With no TV or radio, it was a good way to pass the time (another age-old diversion gave rise to sizable families). Looking back at the number of amicable tricks played on Harry, Joel must've really liked him.

It took a long time and a lot of coaxing before Dad got used to driving up the mountain. "I even began to enjoy the solitude of the hills, unlike the jostling rat race of city traffic," he told me and the kids. I don't know if I believed him, but he claimed that he liked to fetch supplies from Clintwood. He'd come a long way from his first nerve-wracking trek up the mountain.

"There was that one time Joel did play a mean trick on me, though," he said, his eyes distant.

On one particularly hot summer day while the chickens pecked lethargically, the pigs burrowed in the mud, and Bessie the cow shaded herself under the great oak in the front yard, Harry volunteered to run an errand. Grandma needed a bolt of fabric, needles and thread, stove matches, and "one o' them fancy, stainless steel ladles." Grandpa needed a new ax handle and a two-man, crosscut saw.

After getting all the requested supplies in Clintwood, he filled the gas tank and picked up a six-pack of Pabst and a carton of cigarettes (Harry was never any good at rolling his own). Like everyone else, he ran the only stop sign and inched down the narrow road toward the Nealy Ridge turnoff. He was about to turn when he spotted a man with a Scots-Irish profile—all belly and no butt (Joel later made a killing selling suspenders in his Saltville haberdashery).

Joel slapped his battered fedora on his leg, swatted at a yellow jacket, and wiped sweat from his brow. "Hot day, ain't it Harry? Headin' back up ta Ma's?"

"Yep. I'm looking forward to getting up where it's a mite cooler."

"Yeah, it's a scorcher alright. But I don' believe I'd be a-takin' that big ole car up thar just now." Joel turned and gazed uphill while shading his eyes from the blazing sun.

"Huh? Why not?"

"Road's washed out, 'bout halfway up." Joel recapped his balding head and grimaced.

Harry's fear of the treacherous road returned with a vengeance. "It's that bad?" Although proud that he'd conquered the mountain, he wasn't ready to tackle anything out of the ordinary.

"Not a good time ta test yer driving skills. Hillside just gave way a short while ago."

"I really don't want to walk up in this heat." He nodded toward the saw sticking out of his trunk. "And how am I supposed to get back with all this stuff?"

"Wait right here and I'll fetch a way. Can't leave ya lollygagging around town tonight." Joel affected a sympathetic demeanor. "I heard the Coal Black ain't much."

Harry never stopped to consider that the area was experiencing a midsummer drought. He pulled his behemoth Buick into a shaded spot hard by the riverbank where a big flatbed overloaded with lumber was unlikely to hit it.

Joel disappeared down a footpath and returned shortly with a long-eared mule that also didn't want to hike up in the heat. It strained against the rope halter while Joel tugged hard for each stubborn step.

"Ever ride one o' these critters, Harry?" Joel coaxed the mule forward.

Harking back to his racehorses, he stretched the truth. "Nah, but I can ride a horse. He looks fit enough."

"Well, this 'ere brute 'ill git ya where ya wanna go and not fall off them cliffs doin' it."

My uncle had borrowed the most ornery beast he could find in the county. Harry hopped on bareback, almost like he knew what he was doing. When he kicked his ribs, the mule brayed and laid his ears flat, but budged not a step.

"Kick 'em harder, Harry."

Dad laid into the mule. It bucked and swung its head around to nip him. Harry rocked precariously but managed to stay mounted. "Damn it."

"Thought ya could ride, Harry!"

"I can." He kicked with a vengeance while cursing. The beast bared his teeth and tried to take a chunk of his leg, but Harry poked his dress shoe in the animal's face. When the four-legged monster bucked ever higher, Harry's face went pale, then bright red with anger. He kept his seat, but not his cool. "Is this the best damned animal you could find? I thought you had friends around here."

"Not much choice, Harry. I can return 'im if ya like."

"Humph. Guess I'll have to make the best of it."

"Have a good ride." Joel handed Dad a birch switch to whack the mule's backside. He bucked once more, then off they went. "I'll watch yer car for ya," Joel shouted after him. "And I'll bring this stuff up when it's safe."

The city-boy spent that afternoon and early evening whipping, kicking, and cursing the stubborn ass up the mountain.

At dusk, when it began to cool down, Harry rode into Grandpa's barnyard, never having crossed even a hint of washed-out road. Suffering from saddle sores, hoarse from yelling profanities, and caked with dried sweat, he was fit to be tied. "Road's fine," he growled to anyone who would listen.

My wisecracking uncle was no dummy and made himself scarce after he drove Dad's car up late that night. Word spread rapidly on The Ridge and the story got better with each telling. Harry eventually settled down enough to appreciate the humor of it, but he never again quite trusted Joel; that is, until he took a shellacking by playing poker and drinking moonshine with him. White lightning does that to a man.

CHAPTER SIXTEEN

The Gap

F ar down the road from Grandpa's, a dilapidated country store was tucked against a cliff. Hard by its front porch, a narrow mountain lane snaked over a deep crevice. Kids simply called it The Gap, although it probably had a proper name—Mullins Mercantile or Arrington's Appurtenances? Pioneers once purchased essentials at the original log store: wagon repair parts, harnesses, gunpowder and shot, beef jerky, boot soles, and hemp rope. My Scots-Irish forebears who didn't distill their own moonshine bought illicit whiskey stored under the counter.

With the coming of electricity, the newest store boasted a Frigidaire. Cold soft drinks and beer became available, along with tobacco and ammunition. It was also the only store, other than in faraway Clintwood, where kids could buy ice cream, candy bars, and comic books. It beckoned Siren-like to me and my cousins.

One day Bart and David—my Michigan cousins—and I were excused from morning chores. Our moms gave us twenty-five cents apiece, a veritable treasure. We eagerly set out for The Gap, anticipating the highlight of our week.

"Have a good day boys," Grandma said. "Be home in time for supper."

"We will," we said while waving good-bye.

"Watch out for rattlers and copperheads sunning themselves," Grandpa warned while squeezing the cow's teats into a milk pail. For once, he didn't squirt us.

"Okay."

"And be sure to ..." Mom's last admonition faded as we disappeared around the far bend, shuffling along the dirt road and churning up clouds of dust while dreaming of cold treats and sticky sweets.

"Maybe I'll get an ice cream instead of candy," I said.

"Just think, twenty-five cents! That's enough for both candy and pop," Bart exclaimed. *Pop* was Michigander for a soft drink.

David stopped short and pointed to something that caught his eye. "What's that over there?" A decrepit old log barn we'd never noticed was hidden in dense forest.

"Let's check it out," Bart said. Without debate, we sidetracked through an overgrown path. The barn's loading dock, constructed of mill-finished boards, was rotting away. The bulk of the barn that was built with logs, however, was still intact.

Fearlessly, or stupidly, we crawled under the disintegrating deck to investigate scattered mounds of loose red dirt that resembled a Martian landscape. "It's a *doodlebug* city!" I said. Doodlebugs built extensive tunnel systems, much like ants.

We stretched onto our bellies and beckoned the hard-shell, beetle-sized insects with soft rhythmic tones. "Doodlebug, doodlebug, come 'n get your bread and butter. Doodlebug, doodlebug, come 'n get your bread and butter."

"Look! Here comes one." Bart grabbed it.

"There's another one!" David whispered.

The soft intonation actually worked. Scores of armored

insects were soon clamoring out. I scooped up a dozen or so. "What are we gonna do with 'em?"

"I dunno." Bart smiled as one crawled up his arm.

"Ah, heck. Just let 'em go." Older by a year, David was the sensible one.

We scooted out and brushed off the red dust; a mere half hour into our journey and we were already filthy. We continued down the rutted road that wound along Nealy Ridge's crest toward a trove of treats that awaited.

A whitewashed clapboard building, faded and peeling, soon came into sight. The one-room schoolhouse's door didn't have a lock, only a latch, so we ducked inside. The chair-desks, complete with inkwells, were lined neatly in rows, ready for students of all grades to return in the fall. Old *National Geographic* maps, torn and Scotch-taped, lined the walls. Behind the teacher's desk—a plain wooden table—and above a chalkboard, a faded banner demonstrated the art of cursive writing. A birch stick, for pointing and discipline, leaned against an outdated globe in the corner.

In the mid-morning coolness of the darkened room (the storm shutters were closed), I reflected on a pie-eating contest one Christmas. It was highly unusual for my family to visit those treacherous hills when snow-covered, but for some forgotten reason, we had.

Several pies were lined up on the table/desk. Aunt Bessie let me compete with select students while others lined the walls with their parents. She announced, "Put your hands behind your backs," then shouted, "Go!" My face dove into the pie. Everyone cheered their favorites; the joyous noise was deafening.

"Now ... Stop!" Each contestant sat up straight and smiled through a thick layer of glop. I lost—I think I came in last—but it didn't matter, it was a time to remember.

David groused, "Let's get out of here," breaking my reverie.

"Yeah, reminds me too much of school," Bart seconded.

I followed them outside and squinted in the bright glare of an ever-hotter sun.

We next came upon the post office, another faded white clapboard structure, much smaller than the school. We promised our folks we'd pick up the mail since rural delivery was nonexistent. The postmaster was a balding, slight-of-build old coot, whose thick spectacles amplified his bulging eyes. He wasn't always grumpy, but we'd earned a reputation for mischief. As such, many local folks, including this man accountable for the federal mail, considered us unreliable.

He glowered as he pulled a few pieces from the cubby labeled *Counts*, our patronymic. I tugged on the small bundle while he kept a firm hold. "You boys know that tampering with the mail is a *federal* offense."

"Yes, sir." Having seen James Cagney's *Angels with Dirty Faces*, we knew the feds didn't fool around.

"Mrs. Counts is a good friend, known her all my life. You make sure these get to her, safe and sound."

"Oh, we will, sir."

Reluctantly, he parted with the small packet of mail while scolding, "This is serious business, boys. I'll be checking with yer granddaddy next time I see him." He gave us a hard look, surreal through those Coke-bottle glasses.

While backing out the door Bart declared, "It'll get home safe. We promise."

We jumped when the screen door inadvertently slammed behind us. "I thought you had it," I whispered.

"Maybe he did that on purpose," David said.

"Ah, what the heck, he don't like us no way," Bart cavalierly added.

The truth be told, we'd worked hard for our less-than-innocent reputation up on The Ridge. One incident involved fence rails, a horse, and ...

∽

The previous summer Bart, David, and I came up with a grandiose scheme to keep ourselves busy and avoid farm work. "Let's make a log cabin. It'll be our fort." I'm not sure who came up with this idea.

We found Grandpa scattering crushed corn to the chickens in the scratch yard and asked if he knew of a spot where we could build a cabin.

"There's a small clearing about a hundred yards from the house." He pointed down the narrow lane past the dairy cave. "No one goes that-a-way no more. An outhouse used ta be back there."

We continued beyond the privy's ruins, then paced off four walls. Sweating profusely, we chopped at a large tree. It took an hour before it even wobbled. We pushed, but it refused to fall, then we ran into it together. It started to topple, but its branches got entangled in those of its neighbors. "Let's cut this other one so they'll both drop," someone said.

After a third attempt, the trees looked like half-felled dominoes. Fess Parker made it look so easy on TV's *Davy Crockett*.

Finally, the fourth one knocked the others loose, which miraculously landed without killing anyone. Limbing four trees was hard work and our progress was slow.

"At this rate we'll never have enough logs," I moaned.

"How 'bout a small shack?" David suggested.

"Sounds like a plan," I said.

The Ponderosa-sized mansion of our fantasies faded into the ether of a hot sky.

In the meantime, Bart had wandered off and discovered an abandoned paddock enclosed by a split-rail, zigzag fence that weaved like drunken herringbone. A frayed rope held its rickety gate closed. He had a revelation. "Let's use them old rails."

"From the fence?" David wasn't so sure. "What if they belong to someone?"

"I don't think so." Bart was sure. "Heck of a lot easier than cutting down trees." Fences were rare on Nealy Ridge, and this one no longer seemed to serve any purpose.

"We'll just drag 'em up to our cabin," I added. "Easy."

We didn't think to ask if anyone minded; after all, the antebellum fence was falling apart.

Several days later, our cabin walls rose majestically.

David said, "Wind will whip right through it," noting the huge gaps between the irregular logs.

"I know how to make caulk," I volunteered. "Mix clay, sand, and horsehair with water and heat it. It hardens as it cools. Saw it on *Daniel Boone*."

"Does it really work?" David was skeptical.

"I guess."

Bart came to my defense. "Let's at least try."

The following day, Bart and I returned to the partly dismantled paddock to gather hair from posts that horses had used to scratch their haunches. David had gone with Clyde, who had a car, and my brother Lee to get cigarettes and whatever else in Clintwood.

A huge plow horse grazed peacefully nearby, swatting horseflies with his long shimmering black tail. As Bart and I painstakingly plucked small tufts from the splintered wood, he meandered up and nuzzled my hand.

"It's just hair, ole fella, probably yours."

"I guess this paddock is still used," said Bart, stating the obvious. "That's not Grandpa's horse, is it?"

"I don't think so. At least he didn't get loose, but we'd better patch the fence." While jury-rigging the remaining rails, I suggested, "Let's cut some hair off his tail. There's a lot there."

"Sure ... why not?" Bart said agreeably. David wasn't around to talk sense.

"I'll hold his head while you cut," I suggested, being the horse expert.

Bred for heavy labor, the beast's powerful legs were anchored by enormous hooves. Although dwarfed by him, I tightly held onto the leather halter, secretly relieved that Bart had naïvely agreed to play barber near those big hooves.

I rubbed the horse's nose and spoke softly while Bart hacked at his tail with a small penknife. But the puny blade wouldn't cut the tough hair. "I'm gonna run back and hunt around Grandpa's tool shed for something sharper."

"Hurry up, this guy ain't gonna stand here all day," I whispered while patting the animal's brawny neck. He affectionately nuzzled me before easily pulling away to graze.

My crazy cousin returned on the fly, holding high a pair of hedge clippers. "Looky what I found. I'll bet this bad boy will work!" he shouted.

"Shhh." I said, afraid the horse might gallop off. "Don't make so much noise. Let me get a good grip first," like that would make a difference if he bolted.

Bart grabbed his tail and struggled with the clippers while the magnificent equine grazed languidly, unfazed by my feeble attempts to coax his head up. Bart soon had a fist full of hair, which he held aloft with a triumphant grin. "Got it!"

Seems awfully long.

I moseyed back to look at the horse's ass—the animal, not Bart—whose tail was cut off right at the fleshy stub. I was shocked. "Bart, you took the whole damn thing!" He'd also taken away the noble steed's aristocratic grandeur; the poor horse almost looked embarrassed.

"It'll grow back directly," Bart said defensively.

Not that fast.

With ample horsehair to bind our primitive plaster, we filled in the gaps. (We didn't tell David where we got the hair.) The plaster, however, washed out with the first rain. Daniel Boone would've been disappointed in us.

In short order, we were educated about who owned the

horse. Ole man Chadwick wasn't happy when he discovered that "those boys from up North" were responsible for despoiling his handsome workhorse. It had been the county champion for three years running, but now he hid behind the barn, shamefaced. It didn't take home any prizes that year, or the next.

We got a sound thrashing from Grandpa. Mom and Aunt Aida screamed at us too, but I later caught them giggling in private. They didn't like Chadwick any more than other folks on The Ridge. We never finished our cabin.

"C'mon, Carroll. Let's get going." David was anxious to get away from the post office. I stuffed the mail into my back pocket and briskly stepped off the porch. The screen door creaked open behind us. "Ya'll be sure 'n give that mail to yer granddaddy," the postmaster reiterated as a parting shot. His reproaches faded as we practically raced for the hairpin turn ahead.

Farther along the road, we detoured up a steep rocky trail to a fire tower at the base of which was a ranger hut. Its door was locked, so we plastered our faces against the dirty windows to look inside. No personal effects were on the spring bed, and none were hanging on the wooden hooks.

"I don't think anyone's on duty," I mused aloud.

"Let's climb the tower," Bart suggested.

"Yeah, okay." David agreed as long as there was little chance of getting caught.

The tower's rusty struts creaked as we ascended the metal stairs. The upper platform afforded a spellbinding panorama above the treetops; an endless march of majestic peaks jutted above faint blue ridges etched against a distant horizon.

We once climbed this sentinel shortly after dawn. The early-morning light played on a mist that lay gently in the hollows and valleys, the infinite peaks like islands, mirroring the independent spirit of the pioneers, and of those who remained.

In the here and now, time was getting on. After racing down the clanging steps two at a time, we scrambled down the rocky path and continued our trek along the road. Walking at a brisk pace, we kicked up ever more dust while the sun beat fiercely upon the parched road. The Tarzan Swing wasn't far ahead, our last planned detour.

A steep, narrow footpath short-cut a lengthy loop in the road, and near a sharp cliff hung a vine strong enough to support us, yet long enough to trace a wide arc over the chasm. We always had a good swing before our final descent to The Gap, which from up here looked like a model train set with a narrow, tan ribbon of a road.

Standing at the edge of the precipice, Bart firmly grasped the vine with both hands and kicked off. He let out a holler that echoed from the depths while he swung safely back and landed between David and me. "What a gas!" Bart was all grins.

"You're next, David." Bart handed him the vine. Inherently fearful of heights, I was happy to broker any delay.

David took two running steps, pushed off hard, and spewed a brassy yodel that might've been the Rebel Yell. His long legs flailed as he swung farther than Bart. He landed with a victorious smile.

"You guys are too lightweight," he trumpeted while handing me the vine. His cocky grin taunted as if to say, *Go ahead and beat that, little cousin.*

Fear or no, I was determined to outdo them both. I grasped the vine low to lengthen the arc, took an extra step back, and ran forward. Springing catlike, I closed my eyes and left solid ground, pumping my legs to gain altitude. Momentarily weightless at the pinnacle, I knew I'd beaten my cousins. Elated, I swept back toward the cliff, thankful it was all but over.

Then the vine gave way.

I plummeted in a free-fall as my pounding, adrenaline-charged heart smothered what was to be a triumphant cheer. My mind raced. *This is it, the final farewell.*

Suddenly, I slammed hard against the unforgiving rock face, which knocked out what little air remained in my lungs. I crumpled onto a narrow shelf—my lifesaver! Frantically, I tried to breathe, but the air wouldn't come and I almost passed out. With a desperate gasp, I recovered my senses and my breath.

The slender ledge was ten or twelve feet down. I scratched anxiously up toward my waiting cousins who had stretched out flat on the ground to reach for me.

"Grab on, Carroll." David pulled my left wrist.

Bart grabbed my other hand. "We've got you."

Together they dragged me up and over the last jagged foot. I tried to stand, but my legs were weak and quivering, so I sat and nervously dusted off. I looked deep into David's bulging eyes. Genuinely concerned, his face was pale. "You okay?" he asked.

"Uh … yeah. I think so." I'm sure my own face was drained of blood.

Bart just smiled. "That was so cool."

I didn't think it was *cool.* After collecting my senses, I suggested we waste no more time. "We're gonna need plenty of daylight ta git back home." Nealy Ridge was no place to wander around after dark.

I took a couple of drunken steps and pleaded, "Maybe just a second, guys." I plopped onto a boulder to further recover.

While David readily agreed, Bart was antsy, pacing in ever-widening circles and kicking small rocks. "Ouch, damn it." He'd stubbed his toe on a half-buried stone. "Let's dig it out and roll it downhill." He wanted revenge on the rock.

"Sure. I guess there's still time," I acquiesced. Rolling a

stone downhill was a common urchin pastime. It would take but a moment and be ... safe?

We dug with sticks and bare hands. The more we dug, the larger it got, becoming a pretty good-sized boulder. After trenching a sizable moat, we realized it would be far too heavy for us.

The afternoon was slipping away but, determined, we found a limb to use as a lever. It immediately snapped, so Bart found a bigger one and jammed it under the rock. It also broke. We grabbed a lengthy log, so heavy it took two of us to lift.

Sweat streamed down our dusty faces, tracing rivulets of mud until we finally pried the boulder from its ancient tomb. Archimedes would've been proud. When it began to roll toward the cliff, Bart gave it one last kick. The boulder then took on a life of its own. Traveling ever faster, it shot over the edge.

"Wow!" we chimed in unison.

Just when it had begun to roll, billows of dust appeared on the roadbed far below. A four-door sedan, which looked like a matchbox toy, came over the gap.

We stared as the vehicle slowed and came to a stop across from the country store. The car door creaked open. When the driver slammed it shut, the sound echoed through the mountainside. He shuffled across the narrow road and disappeared through the store's creaky screen door.

In the meantime, Bart's geological missile had picked up momentum, recoiling ever higher when hitting obstacles that acted as launch pads. It sped south, loosening pebbles and small stones that trailed in its wake—a mini-avalanche.

Leaps developed into bounds. Saplings that struggled to grow in the rocky cliff face broke like matchsticks. Near the bottom, our boulder bent a small tree, sprung off its top, and landed squarely on the car's roof. The sound of complaining metal reverberated through the valleys.

With one last effort it skidded off the sedan, rolled across the street, and slammed into the store's rickety porch. The mayhem ended in a muffled, anticlimactic thud. Dust, leaves, and small shards of vermin-infested rafter rained softly from the porch roof. If the proprietor had chanced to scan the heights at that moment, he would've seen three wide-eyed delinquents peering down.

"I'm not hungry for any snacks or pop," David muttered. Without further comment, we turned away and headed up the footpath toward home. Our silence was broken only by brief negotiations concerning certain cow paths to take to avoid the road.

We solemnly trudged up the lane to Grandma's house. "So how was your day?" Mom smiled as I handed her the mail.

I shuffled nervously and avoided eye contact. "Okay."

Bart eagerly, maybe too eagerly, added, "It was great!" David kept his head down and mouth shut, announcing a guilt that Mom didn't even suspect.

Sheepishly, I inquired. "Is dinner ready?" After all, we'd worked up a big appetite and hadn't had anything to eat all day.

I sometimes thought about that poor soul and his car. What did he think when he saw his automobile's roof? Did he notice the huge rock lying against the porch? Had he heard anything when it hit? And did he suspect that "those boys from up north" were somehow involved? No one ever asked us about it and we never volunteered the info—until now.

CHAPTER SEVENTEEN

The Trailer

Tania's hygiene patient canceled at the last minute, then mine canceled for the same time slot. This extended the lunchtime by forty-five minutes, a rarity for us.

"Why don't we go out for lunch?" Trish suggested. As we seldom had time to eat out, we jumped at the chance.

We beat the lunch crowd by twenty minutes and enjoyed a relaxing meal. Stuffed and happy, we left the restaurant with plenty of time before the afternoon onslaught. My car reverberated with laughter on the way back to the office, but when I turned into our driveway, the chatter abruptly died. About halfway up the hill, an enormous mobile home partially blocked our lane.

"What's that, Dr. C?"

"Sure is big," Trish noted.

"Wasn't there when we left," Tania said.

"When'd you order a secondhand home?" Kate goaded.

"I didn't," I said with a bark upon noticing their grins in the rearview mirror.

Lee!

While I maneuvered my four-wheel drive onto the grass, slick from recent rains, Lee, my older brother, bounded out, waving and smiling. It wasn't the small camper or pickup he normally drove; rather, it was a rust and primer-gray tenement-on-wheels. Remember Eddie in *Christmas Vacation*? This huge monster was worse.

Back on solid pavement, I looked behind me and nearly collided with an eight-wheel diesel pickup parked catawampus and center stage in the patient lot. Patients wouldn't be able to park, assuming they made it past the trailer.

It had started innocently enough ...

The previous Monday morning, Lee phoned from his home near Bristol. "I'm-a coming up for a visit. Be thar later today." Even though we were raised in the DC suburbs, Lee thought of himself as a backwoods pioneer. To hear him tell it, he was "born-n-raised a mountain man, jus' like grandpappy."

Having spent our formative summers on Grandpa's primitive homestead, we mimicked the mannerisms and speech of Nealy Ridge hill folk. I'd since lost most of my accent, but Lee remained a free spirit and moved down to that area, where he thought he might fit in. I couldn't fault him for craving a simpler lifestyle. Unlike many baby boomers, he knew where to find solitude.

As a youngster, Lee liked to have fun and laughed a lot—a happy-go-lucky guy. But while most folks only saw his lighter side, a darkness lurked deep within. He had his demons to fight.

Within our modest Maryland ranch home, a short, narrow hallway connected three small bedrooms. Our only phone—a rotary—was parked in a nook along that wall, which backed up to Lee's room. Mom would stretch the cord and sit on the floor for conversations, all of which were long. He once over-

DR. CARROLL JAMES

heard Mom saying, "Rita, our sons do get along so well. Such gay fellows, especially Lee."

Lee came barreling out of his room, his perpetual smile replaced by a scowl. "Momma! Don't say that. "Gay" doesn't mean what you think it means."

"Oh, nothing Rita," our mother continued. "It's just that Lee hates it when I tell folks how gay he is." There was no convincing the backwoods gal. Her mother was born in the nostalgic Gay Nineties and Mom saw such happy traits in her eldest son. I, on the other hand, was a serious kid, born old.

Although raised in a lower-middle-class family, Lee looked deep within and found a rugged antebellum sort. Most of his shenanigans—and mine—were innocent enough. In our knife-throwing phase, for example, we made a shambles of the family picnic table, splintering it with our huge Bowie knives. If we'd thought it through, we would've tipped the table over and used the underside with little fault. We weren't evil, just stupid. But Dad wasn't real happy about it.

Sadly, over the years Lee devolved into a hard-drinking miscreant. I couldn't blame the War for all his problems, but Vietnam did take its toll. Self-destructive, he left behind a string of girlfriends, wives, and more than a few dogs that Mom ultimately cared for, filling his life with philandering. Before winter hit, he'd shack up with some drunken tattooed lady he'd met in a bar. That might last until spring when she'd kick his "lazy butt" out.

Summer often found him in a small tent with nothing but dogs for company. In defiance of park regulations along the C&O Canal, they were never leashed. This independence deluded him into thinking he was a modern-day Daniel Boone.

Throughout the years, he went through vehicles the way people go through potato chips. Every car and truck was totaled or repossessed. A dog or two, or several—and maybe a couple of tomcats—invariably rode around with him. Most of his pickups were fitted with a cap, inside of which he'd set up house.

Parking helter-skelter to show off his latest vehicle, Lee proudly exclaimed, "Ain't she a beaut, Carroll?" The rust, dents, bald tires, cracked windshield, broken headlight(s), and missing tailpipe didn't jive with "a beaut." A car wash might've helped a little. A good scrubbing wouldn't have hurt Lee, either.

"Picked me up a cat from the Berkeley Springs pound," Lee announced. "Rides in the back to keep mice outta my vittles." Lee grabbed the tailgate's rusty latch and yanked hard; it swung open with a spine-tingling screech. Slimy globs of fur lay on the floor. "Well, looky thar. She spit all them kittens out on the way here. Guess she ain't no tomcat. Shouldn't a named her Clyde."

Six suckling's were gathered around Clyde's swollen teats, nursing and making biscuits while sprawled on one of Lee's better flannels (meaning it had no holes). Lee tottered beside the truck, a beer in one hand and a cigarette in the other, the proud father grinning ear to ear.

Old before his time, he became more aimless than a free spirit. In fact, it was hard to be around him sometimes. But the old joy occasionally surfaced, which was when Kate and I enjoyed his company.

As the years lengthened and our grandparents passed away, the farm was sold. One by one, my relatives moved to metropolitan areas and we no longer headed south every summer. Our second cousins began sponsoring reunions to rectify this drift from family roots. A beautiful, heavily wooded park near Bristol became the gathering place.

Lee and I had busy lives. Well, I did anyway, and I failed to make the first reunion, but Lee managed to tear himself away. He simply packed up the tent, the cooler, and the dog(s) and headed south. When I later visited him in Hedgesville, West Virginia, all he could talk about was the reunion.

Not only had he become reacquainted with great aunts,

uncles, second cousins, and childhood friends after a twenty-year absence, he married one. And not one of the old friends. The blushing bride was my second cousin, and his. I heard comic Jeff Foxworthy in my mind: "You might be a redneck if you go to family reunions to pick up chicks."

It was love at second sight. Jinni-Lee's name added an interesting twist; both kissing cousins sported the general's patronymic. She accepted his proposal, and they were married within the week.

Neither of them was the same person they were growing up—and they couldn't have been more different. Only after Vietnam did Lee earn his GED, while Jinni-Lee was an accomplished pediatric nurse, tending critically ill children in a major Bristol hospital. All too often, however, intelligence had little bearing on common sense. She failed to think through the implications of this mismatched marriage.

Jinni-Lee sold her home in Abingdon and bought an older house in Bristol. Lee contributed dogs and put his name on the deed, promising to get a job as soon as "one opened up."

At some point, Kate and I visited them. An old oak tree shaded a cozy wraparound porch, which leaned a little to the left. A rickety, double-door shed was packed with yard equipment, including several wheelbarrows and two riding mowers. "Momma bought me a new one as a wedding present," Lee said, hopping on and proudly driving the mower around his small yard.

"The old one doesn't work?" I shouted over the noise of the diesel engine.

"Works fine, but I wanted a powerful one."

Their quarter-acre lot was fenced with cattle wire on three sides and a faded picket fence along the street. Lee hadn't gotten around to painting it. The lawn was mainly tree roots and ruts dug by the dogs. *So why two riding mowers?* The larger question was why he needed one at all; it was all trim work.

Lee turned off the mower and left it in the front yard, motioning for us to follow him up the back porch steps. The screen door slammed shut as I tripped over a cardboard box of newborn kittens. (Lee had cut out one side of the box so they could come and go.) Jinni-Lee emerged from her vintage 1940s kitchen and gave us a warm hug. "Don't just stand out here, Carroll. Come right on in, Kate. Lee, I thought I told you to put those cats in the shed."

"They don't like it out thar."

I wondered how he knew that.

Scads of family photos were displayed on the end tables, coffee table, window ledges, and fireplace mantel. They over-flowed onto nightstands, dressers, and kitchen counters, giving the place a homey, yet cluttered touch. Along with her mis-matched family antiques, and a few yard sale items of Lee's, Jinni-Lee had lovingly decorated their home in hillbilly eclectic.

Not since childhood had Lee experienced such down-home domesticity. Better yet, unlike with his numerous other wives and live-ins, he'd never seemed so genuinely content. She was good for my brother, and I was happy for him. He'd even sworn off alcohol—supposedly.

While leisurely gazing around the living room, my eyes rested on one particular set of pictures. On the mantel, a double-framed set prominently displayed the newlyweds' high school photos. A chill shot up my spine; they looked like twins. I couldn't stop staring at their identical light blue eyes, which seemed to stare back into my soul.

While they talked and laughed with Kate, I noticed that they acted alike. In addition, Jinni-Lee's hair had begun to grey and thin, like Mom's—and Lee's. Upon closer inspection, I realized there was only one way to tell them apart quickly: he was the one with the beard. It was a little creepy.

In deference to Kate's asthma, Lee and I stepped out back so he could smoke, although stale tobacco permeated the house. Between long drags and perfectly round smoke rings that drifted through the hot Southern air, Lee said, "We enjoy the same things: bowlin', campin', drag races, movies"—my brother never cared a fig about the flicks until now—"eatin' out with friends, or just watchin' TV." He smiled. "We were meant for each other, Carroll. It's like ... well, Jinni-Lee and I have so much in common."

"Yeah, like your genes," I blurted without thinking.

After an awkward silence, he mustered a hearty laugh and blew another smoke ring. I could swear it was heart-shaped.

Winter came and went; a warm spring promised a hot summer. When Lee called that Monday morning around five, he announced, "I'll be up thar today. Want ta show off my new five-wheel trailer. I need ta get away fer a spell." I thought moving down home *was* getting away. He also planned to spend a little time with his two daughters, products of two previous relationships. Although Jinni-Lee made a good living, he was short of money so the call was collect. Maybe the honeymoon was over.

I had learned to never expect Lee until I saw him coming, although I had a gut feeling he'd show up this time; he hadn't seen his girls since his latest nuptials. That evening, he called from a truck stop.

"Hey little bro'. It's takin' longer than I thought. This twenty-eight-foot gooseneck is slowing me down." *It's twenty-eight feet long?* "I'm gonna spend the night on the road. Got a bedroom, kitchen, and living room with TV and easy chair." *All the comforts of home.* "Be thar sometime tomorrow, early afternoon if my old F350 holds up."

That was a potential problem. Tomorrow I'd be tied up with patients and the parking lot would be packed. "I might be busy, Lee, when you get here. Just pull your rig onto the gravel out by the shed. You can tap into electric and water out there. After work, I'll help you."

"No problem-o, bro'. Can't wait fer ya ta see it." The trailer was his latest pride and joy. He never mentioned Jinni-Lee.

The next morning, our two cancellations were a welcome reprieve, and I'd totally forgotten about Lee when we left for lunch. Now, he was blocking the driveway and parking lot just when a whole slew of patients was expected.

Hopping out of my Jeep, I ran down our tree-lined lane while the staff continued to giggle. Lee had set up a small chain-link fence in our front yard. This makeshift dog pen was propped up by a few limbs the trailer had knocked off our maple trees.

When I reached to shake his hand, Lee wrapped me in a bear hug, something we never did. He hadn't bathed for quite some time; stale beer and tobacco oozed from his pores. I felt like I needed another shower before seeing patients.

"Look inside 'er. Got lots of room," he said proudly with a grin.

I'll bet. It took up half the lane and part of the front yard. I didn't mean to be abrupt, but I was. "Lee. You gotta git that thing out of the way. People can't hardly squeeze by. Take it on up the hill." My diction reverted to my mountain heritage.

"Gotta let Winston take a leak first." *Winston?* His mutt proceeded to kill a patch of grass. The pug looked more like a gremlin mated with ... maybe a bat? After taking care of business, he jumped into the truck's cab while Lee re-hitched his mobile home. It took interminable maneuvering before he got it backed onto the gravel and out of the way.

Breathing a sigh of relief, I briskly walked to the office while our first afternoon patient drove up. I called over my right shoulder, "I'll see ya soon as I'm done with work. We'll have plenty a time to talk later." He'd started to level the behemoth for what appeared would be an extended stay.

I stored a forest-green Boy Scout trailer unobtrusively by the shed. I figured Lee's trailer wouldn't look so bad next to the little eight-foot pull-behind.

I figured wrong.

Lee's rig dwarfed it and the bulky hitch overhung the asphalt by about eight feet. Not only that, but its industrial leg made a deep depression in my pavement. He backed his disengaged F350 against my shed's double doors, completely blocking them. The three vehicles—Boy Scout trailer, Ford pickup, and mobile home—had all the markings of a junkyard. They also defined an asymmetrical, gravel courtyard whose open end faced the dental office.

Before burying my head in the first gaping mouth of the afternoon, I took time to gaze out the window and watch Lee establish his campsite.

First, he fetched the dog pen. He could've placed it behind the tall shrubs bordering the parking lot where it'd be out of sight. Not a chance. Instead, he set it on the gravel as the courtyard's centerpiece. The crushed blue stone seemed a little rough for a dog—grass would be nicer—but Lee already had a solution: a tattered, smelly, flea-infested carpet remnant.

Next, he unfolded an aluminum camp table onto which he placed a rusted hibachi. Then he unrolled a huge awning that stretched the length of his multicolored tenement. Unlike the RV Frank and I had rented, its fabric was mostly intact.

Lee strategically placed a tattered lawn chair beside a cooler. *Why a cooler? Isn't there a refrigerator?* He disappeared inside and came back with a six-pack—he wouldn't have to get his butt out of the chair to retrieve a frosty brew. A threadbare welcome mat landed at the foot of the stairs, contributing to the illusion of a KOA.

While I watched, Trish called to me, "Doog waiting, Docteur."

I wonder how Doug is taking this, I thought. Trish looked

out the window, then became as mesmerized as I was. I finally tore myself away and went to numb up Doug. "Just relax for a few minutes. I'll be back shortly." He wasn't nervous; the scene outdoors preoccupied him.

When I returned to the observation window to see what Lee was up to now, Trish hadn't moved. Lee again disappeared into the depths of his shack-on-wheels and reappeared with an American flag. He duly attached it to the awning's corner pole with duct tape. Despite the appalling reception he'd received upon returning from Vietnam, he was patriotic to the core.

As already suggested, he probably hadn't bathed for several days—Lee, not the dog. Winston had never been washed. And neither dog's nor master's hair had been trimmed for months. Lee's stringy gray mane complemented his ZZ Top beard, and a filthy, tattered T-shirt didn't quite cover his ample beer belly. His cutoff jeans sagged loose in the butt while two hairy twig-legs struggled to balance his top-heavy gut.

Like me, Lee had no heinie to speak of. For untold generations, belts or suspenders had been necessities in my maternal family—Uncle Joel's haberdashery was well-stocked with them. So why in the name of propriety had Lee failed to wear either? Inevitably, the cutoffs drifted south while he set up camp. When both hands were occupied in raising the flag, his shorts began their march to Georgia, only to be yanked north just in the nick of time.

Whenever he retrieved his rat-dog from that homemade kennel, Lee had to bend over the makeshift fence—way over. *Must he aim his butt at the office every time?* When placed back into the pen, Winston scooted his hind end across the carpet sample. Worms—nice touch.

We were busy, and cars became bottle-necked in the driveway. Although still prominent, the mobile home was at least out of the way. *He is family ... and how much worse can it get?* I reasoned.

"Hey," announced one patient, "that old guy in the lawn chair looks like Dr. James." Lee's butt hung through the lounge chair's plastic straps while he drank a beer. A faded baseball cap shaded his eyes. *Maybe Kate's right; it's time to trim my beard.*

When Sarah, my travel companion in the USSR, arrived for her scheduled checkup, she said, "Hey, Dr. C. Did you know you've got a homeless man living in your driveway?"

I chuckled. "Maybe you can ask him to fire up the barbecue. The hot dogs should be ready by the time you're finished."

"Swell, does the price include a beer?"

"Sure. Ask for a number three, and he'll throw in a small bag of chips."

"Sold." Sarah was a good sport.

Soon after, a new patient came up the drive, stopped and stared, then immediately left. I don't think she ever came back.

The afternoon progressed in like fashion until a proper yet pleasant young mom of Scandinavian heritage arrived with her three young kids, all girls, all blonde, all blue-eyed, and all in frilly skirts. Although I'd been seeing them for a couple of years, I didn't know them well.

Her youngest had just taken a nasty fall and whacked her front tooth on the sidewalk. Despite our busy schedule, we squeezed her in and Trish took her right back. The kid's gums oozed blood around the displaced baby tooth. After taking an X-ray and cleaning it with three percent hydrogen peroxide, I escorted mother and daughter to the waiting room.

"You can wait comfortably out here while the film develops," I suggested. "It'll just be a few minutes. I want to be sure that the permanent tooth underneath isn't damaged."

When I held the door for them, we were immediately insulted by the rank odor of tobacco mixed with stale beer and body odor. Lee was slouched comfortably in a leather chair, his feet splayed against the folks waiting on either side of him. Thumbing through a magazine, he scratched first one armpit, then the other. *I hope he doesn't go for the crotch*, I thought.

By that point, patients had had plenty of time to inspect the wealth of tattoos adorning his arms and legs. When Lee was a teenager, Cousin Clyde tattooed a pair of dice on his left forearm with a sewing needle dipped in India ink and heated by a cigarette. Being quite artistic, Lee later added Pepé Le Pew. During his stint in the army, Goofy, dressed in fatigues, was carved by a professional. The caption read, "Never Again." My personal favorite, though, was the Playboy Party Girl, seductively poised on his right shoulder. In polite company he'd discreetly cover certain body parts with Band-Aids, which he forgot today.

The blonde mom's smile turned into a frown as she stepped into the waiting room and with lightning speed, gathered her other daughters under her wings. The injured tot, feeling much better now, wriggled loose and skipped over to the window. The mongrel Winston was scooting its butt across the carpet sample.

"Hey look, a dawg!"

Single-minded, the cute little girl bolted for the outside door. Without releasing her other charges, mom tackled her and tucked her safely away with the older ducklings. It was a miracle more teeth weren't damaged in the fray. The four of them settled into two chairs as far from Lee as they could get. The saving grace was Kate's familiar face behind the reception counter.

Lee, the shady-looking mountain man, suddenly popped up from his chair, scaring the family half to death, and declared, "I'm a-takin' one of bro's magazines to the lib'ary, if'n ya knows what I mean. Heh, heh."

Tucking a *People* under one arm, he sauntered out the door and across the parking lot, then disappeared into his trailer. The clustered blue-eyed family now knew that he and

I were related, spawned from the same line. My off-the-cuff comment about Jinni-Lee and Lee's genes came back to haunt me.

Once he was gone, mom relaxed her grip enough for the kids to again breathe freely. I retrieved the X-ray, but also grabbed my camera with a zoom lens. "Let me get a picture of this." I stood in the doorway and took a great shot before telling the mom the good news about her daughter's tooth. "It'll be fine, just a little TLC for a couple days."

She grinned and thanked me before herding her brood into the family van. I think she saw the humor in it, but she still kept one eye fixed on the camper all the while.

The afternoon was drawing to a close when Phil (my attorney and friend who had muddied his white slacks at our Christmas Eve brunch that one year—see book one, *I Swear to Tell the Tooth*), arrived for his biannual checkup. With a keen legal eye, he scrutinized the bizarre scene. "There's gotta be some money in this."

He was joking, but I was still thankful he hadn't witnessed the pretty little girls clinging desperately to their mother. Despite their experience, that family remained loyal patients. They did, in fact, have a good a sense of humor like most of my patients. They had to.

When the workday finally ended, I ambled over to Lee's homestead. He confessed that he and Jinni-Lee were having marital troubles. "Jus' need some time apart." When I mentioned that we weren't ready to start a KOA, he promised to only stay through the weekend.

Actually, this mini-reunion was long overdue, and we had a good visit once the office closed for the weekend. My nieces stopped by and spent a couple nights in the trailer while Lee slept soundly outside under the stars with Winston, his pioneering soul expressing itself.

∞

Two weeks later, Lee left. Despite his garish campground display, he did clean up after himself. I discovered several overstuffed Hefty bags stacked behind the shed—they were mainly full of beer cans, but one was squishy and smelled of dog poop. A large oil spot remained where the truck had been parked, though. He couldn't have known ... and I grew not to care.

CHAPTER EIGHTEEN

Kate Goes to Mexico

The ancient Boeing 727 raced down a bumpy runway toward a towering mountain. It took off, violently buffeted by erratic wind currents, and banked steeply to clear the crest. Kate anxiously glanced at Joel, our seven-year-old, seated between us. White-knuckled, she looked over and fixed me with a glacier-melting glare.

"We'll be there soon." I patted Joel's knee, which was false bravado. I hated flying.

After our plane touched down in Veracruz, a mobile staircase slammed against the fuselage. Searing heat hit us when the cabin door opened. Perspiring profusely, I ran over and grabbed our luggage before it stuck to the asphalt. "We get our bags out here," I explained. "Airport's not very busy."

"So why do you think that is, Carroll? Maybe 'cause there's not much here?" Kate fired back. Dripping with perspiration, she swatted a mosquito that left a splotch of blood on her arm. Joel squinted in the bright sunshine and scratched his sweaty neck.

∽

It all started when I returned from Oaxaca the first time. My photos of impoverished children with ragged grins tugged at Kate's maternal heartstrings. "How 'bout joining me on another trip?" I casually suggested.

"What could I do? I'm not a nurse."

"You could organize my clinic. The Indians tend to wander off after they get numb, before I treat them. When it wears off, they return mad as hornets." ("Medicine no damn good," Bob had translated. He hadn't included the expletive, but to look at them, I think that's what they actually said.)

"You could keep them in line until I pull their tooth," I suggested.

Kate's enthusiasm waned. "I guess ..."

"And clean instruments."

Her face fell further. "Yeah ..."

Think, Carroll! "The kids love to sing, play games, and make crafts." With that I hit a home run. She beamed that bright-eyed twinkle I love.

"Joel could also entertain them," I suggested.

Her smile disappeared—*swing and a miss.* "It'd be a great life experience for him," I added, encouraging her to think it over. After praying about it, both Kate and our blue-eyed towhead decided to go.

"They'll touch you a lot," I warned Joel. "But it's just because they're curious. You'll get used to it." I decided not to tell him that they sometimes plucked my leg hairs.

"I can handle it, Dad," he reassured me—and himself.

I whispered to Kate, "They're gonna be on him like stink on manure. Many have never seen a white kid." *Or a white woman*, I didn't add. She frowned.

We missed our connection in Dallas, forcing us to spend the night in Mexico City. The hotel was almost clean; I could smell the disinfectants. The bed was comfortable, the shower hot, and the toilet had a seat, unlike many in the airport.

During our turbulent flight to Veracruz, the guy across the aisle lit up a cigarette and casually flicked ashes in the general direction of his ashtray, which was stuffed full with used gum. Kate fanned the air and squirmed.

"At least the onboard bathrooms are functional," I said with an uncomfortable smile.

"Not the one back there," she gestured.

I was thankful when we finally arrived in Veracruz, only one day late. After calling Bob, I told Kate, "He can't pick us up until later today."

"Another delay," Kate grumbled.

I had to think of something. "What do you say we check out the beach and have lunch there?" Kate tried to smile, but there was no twinkle. She and Joel were game for anything other than hanging out in the stifling terminal. And Veracruz's coastline had the allure of a Paradise Lost.

We retrieved swimsuits from our bags, stuffed the luggage into a locker, and hailed a cab. Over the roar and knock of the engine, I shouted to the driver, "Where's *su mer*?"

"*Qué?*" he stared.

When I realized that *mer* was French, I tried again. "You know, *agua*."

"*Sí. Agua.*" He offered his half empty water bottle, sitting on the cab's grimy console.

"No," I shouted. "The ocean, the shore, the Gulf of Mexico."

"Ah. *El* ..."

I couldn't hear the rest—mufflers were as rare as toilet seats —but replied, "*Sí.*"

He floored the wreck and slowly accelerated to a break-neck speed. That was Kate's first introduction to travel by car, south of the border. Stoplights were mere warnings; drivers sped up to clear the intersection before the other guy. There wasn't always a winner.

"Well, at least we're heading east, toward the coast," I said with a smile. Kate's eyes burned a hole in the back of my head while Joel's Game Boy beeped repeatedly—he'd gone to a happy place. Thankfully, the resort was close.

Resort?

We screeched to a halt below a huge, neon sign that read *La Mamba*, which towered over the hotel and was backlit by the morning sun. The place seemed nice enough, in a gaudy way. I gave the cabbie a generous tip. He flashed a gold-capped grin before puttering away, trailing a cloud of black exhaust.

In the cavernous lobby, a guard eyed us suspiciously. I went straight to the desk and asked if we could use the beach.

"*Qué?*" The clerk looked puzzled.

"*Agua?*" That had worked before, sort of.

"*Sí, agua.*" He snapped his fingers and a bellboy ran off, returning shortly with three sealed bottles, which I gratefully accepted.

I looked toward an enormous window overlooking the shore and pointed. The bellboy smiled. "Ah. *Sí, sí.*" He took Kate's arm and escorted us to a huge deck packed with revelers dancing to a deafening mariachi band.

Spiked heels, tight dresses, and bright makeup were all the rage with the ladies. Guys sported cowboy hats, pointy boots, and pastel shirts unbuttoned to their navels. Come to think of it, the gals' tops also dipped pretty low.

Kate, Joel, and I were in T-shirts, shorts, and flip-flops.

A man swirled a mixed drink and smiled at Kate before looking me over top to bottom with a grimace. I walked up to him and gestured toward the beach. He didn't understand. Joel, who knew a little Spanish, tried to help but couldn't be heard over the blaring music.

A woman approached. "Are you lost?" Her English was perfect. "Help yourselves to the food and drink."

"We came for the beach," I explained. *I've got to learn the language.*

"We have something better." She grabbed my hand and led me to a plywood cage with fake bars where a stripe-shirted cashier wore a cheesy visor. "This is play money. Gambling before noon is illegal," she said with a wink. I then noticed the blackjack tables, roulette wheels, and papier-mâché horse heads on poles used on the fake racetrack.

"Thanks." We accepted a wad of funny money and filled up on hors d'oeuvres before discovering stairs that led down to the shore. We ducked into the restrooms to change into swimsuits and soon joined the families frolicking on the beach. There were more than a few dogs catching Frisbees or digging in the sand, and Joel and I played in the mild surf while Kate snapped a few photos.

"I'm gonna keep your mom company for a bit," I said, wading onto the darkish granular sand. "Don't go too far out, buddy."

"I won't," Joel said before diving under a wave.

Holding hands, Kate and I strolled slowly along the beach. Things were looking up ... until I noticed a huge trench coursing through the sand. On closer inspection, I saw that a drainage pipe from the city emptied into it. The wind shifted and confirmed my worst fears—the sludge mingled with the surf, turning the sand a slight brown. Yuk!

"Joel! Get out of there. NOW! That water's full of cra ... uh, mud!" We bolted for the restrooms and cleaned up as best we could. When we met back in the lobby, Kate glared another hole through me. I began to feel like Swiss cheese. "*Aeropuerto. Pronto*," I told a cabby.

We returned to the hot terminal and silently waited for Bob. Thankfully, he soon pulled up in his familiar Suburban, screeching to a halt out front. The brakes still worked.

His sunburnt visage was a welcome sight. "So, Carroll, this is the little woman?"

"Yep. Kate, meet Bob," I said while his fleshy paws enveloped her hand. Bob was his jolly self, which made Kate smile, despite the "little woman" appellation. Everyone liked Bob; he could make Scrooge laugh.

"Welcome to Mexico, Kate. And who's this fine young lad?"

"This is Joel, our youngest," Kate beamed.

"Well, it's great to meet you, Joel." Bob gave him a hearty, man-sized handshake.

We tossed our packs into the four-wheel drive and headed south down that narrow ribbon of potholed asphalt they called a highway. Kate squirmed; the seat's springs still poked. "You okay back there? You can sit up here if you want," I offered.

"We ... we almost hit that truck head on," she stammered. "No! I don't want to sit up there."

I'd failed to warn her about the game of chicken that everyone else took for granted. *I hope we arrive before dark when it gets really dicey*, I thought.

"Kate, see that overloaded mango truck?" Bob said. "It'll take days to get there if we don't pass it." About that time the sky clouded up and a fine mist gently fell. We slid a bit on the wet road while passing the next truck.

I tried a distraction. "How's that Game Boy, son?"

Kate seethed. "You woke him up."

I hadn't realized he could sleep in the chaos.

Bob talked nonstop, either not hearing our bickering or simply ignoring it. Finally, we arrived at dusk. "Welcome to Mission Tuxtepec," he said.

Ignoring the drizzle, Flo came outside to greet Kate, who nodded but didn't say much, still in shock from the fright-ride.

"And this must be the young man we've heard so much about." Flo smiled at Joel, who simply acknowledged her with a sleepy grin.

Their second-floor flat wasn't as hot as I remembered, although the tiny kitchen was, since Flo was always boiling water. With the long trip behind us, Kate relaxed in the glow of her hospitality. "Come on in. I want you to meet the two young ladies you'll be traveling with."

We crammed around the small kitchen table to meet Ruth, a dental technician from the United Kingdom whose cockney was hard to decipher, and Ann, an assistant from Belgium who spoke what I thought was perfect English.

"Ou, tis 'ot 'n 'ere," Ruth declared.

"What?"

"We b' sweatin' like buggers." Ruth fanned herself with a napkin.

"Oh, yeah," I said, "but you get used to it. Evenings aren't bad, but watch out when the sun climbs high—you'll be searching for shade."

"Ca' na b' Lancashire sumr."

"I … guess." Like I understood.

Ann quietly took it all in while we ate dinner.

Afterwards, Kate and I took an evening stroll to cool off. The resident girls, going about their chores, greeted us with broad smiles. "*Buenas tardes.*" Kate's heart melted when she heard them singing. Back in the barracks-style room, Kate, Joel, and I fell fast asleep despite the heat, humidity, and groaning whirr of the ceiling fan.

At five in the morning, the sun was little more than a faint glow on the horizon, and the lilting strains of worship songs floated on the cool morning air. "Carroll. I had no idea how pleasant waking up could be," Kate said, enraptured.

At breakfast, Bob outlined our trip. "We'll go to a hydro-electric dam and catch a skiff. Pack mules will be waiting upriver where it gets shallow. Depending on how many there are, some of us will ride and the rest will walk from there. We'll spend the night in Usila before continuing on to Tejas."

"Why don't we hop a puddle jumper, like last year?" I suggested.

"Times are hard, donations down." Bob remained upbeat. "Let's go, everybody. *Vámonos.*"

The Suburban had been stuffed with supplies and interpreters, so Joel sat in the back on his Mom's lap while I hopped into the front seat. A huge Mexican straddled the console, his cheeks spilling onto me and Bob. Flo squeezed in next to me. I don't know how she closed the door, or how Bob shifted gears between that Mexican's beefy legs.

The helpers in back sang boisterously during the cramped, half-hour ride. Their mood was infectious, and Bob, who couldn't carry a tune, sang just as loud. While humming and grinning, he turned into a steep, bone-rattling lane that led down to the lake's makeshift dock.

"Let's go. Sun's gonna git hot." He climbed out and beat the dust from his jeans with his cap. Several men were loitering by the boat launch. "Hey, *amigos*, little help here?"

Our leaky skiff was packed to the gunwales. We climbed aboard and the captain pushed off with a wooden paddle. He fired up the Johnson outboard and it chugged to life, propelling us across the placid water, which glistened in the low sun.

Joel gawked wide-eyed at the approaching jungle as we entered the Usila River and left civilization behind. About midmorning, he dug into his backpack for peanut butter crackers. Bob grinned.

"I love those things. Pass 'em around," Bob said. Joel thought he was joking.

He wasn't.

I leaned over and whispered, "Go ahead and share them, son."

He reluctantly handed the package to the man beside him. After making the rounds, only one cracker was left for Joel. "Everything's shared," I said. He shrugged and devoured it, washing it down with water from his sports bottle. I took a swig from my round metal canteen—old-school.

As the river narrowed, overhanging boughs provided some respite from the sun. We caught glimpses of colorful, exotic birds squawking in the treetops. Lizards scampered through the ferns and up trees while iguanas lazed on the higher limbs. Howler monkeys protested.

Our skiff shuddered when the propeller scraped bottom. "Everyone out," Bob bellowed. "Grab your water." We waded toward the riverbank and hiked along a trail while two men pulled the lightened boat upstream.

"It's cooler under the trees," Kate noted before we hopped aboard, where the river deepened. We scraped bottom a few more times, then hiked between channels until the skiff was beached at a sunbaked clearing. Several trails branched out from the crossroads.

Myriad people and animals were crowded into the clearing, and canoes and dugouts lined the muddy banks. Crates of soft drinks and beer were randomly stacked among bulging burlap bags. Burros, mules, and horses stomped while their tails swatted at big ugly flies. Donkeys kicked at anyone within range. The locals yelled and kicked back.

"Reminds me of a bus terminal," I mumbled.

"Check this out, Dad. Cokes!"

"You might want to stick to water, Joel."

Bob looked around. "Let me see if I can scrounge a few more animals."

No luck. He dug out a plastic bag of raisin oatmeal cookies. "Flo cooked 'em last night after ya'll went to bed."

I took a couple and passed them to Joel, who warily shook his head. "Listen, buddy. I know you don't like oatmeal, and I don't like raisins. But this is probably lunch. Eat up."

Bob overheard, so to make them more palatable, he traded cookies for Cokes from a drover. Joel eagerly gulped and immediately spit it out. "It's hot!"

"Dry oatmeal and hot Coke ... it doesn't get much better

than this," I said, straight-faced. Not amused, Joel drank his warm water.

While Bob pondered how to divvy up our crew, I whispered to him. "Kate has asthma. She should ride, but don't tell her I asked." He nodded and quietly assigned Kate, Joel, and Ann to burros. Bob, Ruth, and I would walk. The two groups, each with guides and interpreters, would take different routes.

Kate protested. "You and Joel will be fine," Bob reassured her. "We'll take shortcuts that horses can't negotiate. We'll all get to Usila about the same time this evening."

Kate reluctantly mounted her mule. Joel beamed while they forded a wide tributary of the Usila River. "See ya later, Dad."

"Catch you in Usila," I shouted before turning into a dark jungle trail. As the hours went by, I found it hard to keep up with our guides, who had unlimited energy. Ruth also fell behind, but we caught up with everyone at a small village of five thatched-roof huts where Bob was seated on a log in the shade. "Have a sit-down and rest, guys."

"Sounds good." I was bushed.

"An' me legs 'r sore." Ruth wasn't shy about complaining.

"Let's polish off the cookies." Bob held out the bag. I chased one with a greedy swig of water that ran down my neck, which in the heat felt good.

An old guy in rags hobbled by. That is, I think he was old; it was hard to tell under his grimy whiskers. He paused, eyeballed us, and shuffled over. Pulling up his trousers, he showed Bob his bleeding leg. Through our interpreter—the man only spoke Chinentaco—he said that he'd accidentally sliced himself with a machete. The nasty gash was infected.

"How about cleaning and stitching it, Dr. C?" No one cared that I was only a dentist. The old guy never flinched while I sutured.

"*Gracias, señor.*" He did know that much Spanish. I gave

him an envelope of antibiotics and he limped away, disappearing between two huts.

As we stood to leave, he returned with a fresh bunch of bananas, smaller but fruitier than what we were used to in the States. "Oh ho," Bob said, laughing. "Kate and Joel don't know what they're missing."

Refreshed, our small group took off at a fast pace, but I soon slowed down. "Isn't the scenery beautiful?" I said.

While Ruth and I lingered, our guides continued along the trail and I lost track of Bob. Ruth and I were alone in the jungle.

"I'm sure the Indians will wait for us, but we'd better get moving."

"Ou … wa' way?" Ruth pointed to a side trail.

"This way seems to be the main road to Usila," I said.

Unaccustomed to the jungle—she came from London—she grew more nervous with each exhausting step. Pretty comfortable in the woods, I tried to ease her mind.

"We'll be fine, Ruth."

Just then, the trail split equally.

"Now wha'?" Ruth sounded scared … or ticked off.

"You go a hundred yards up that trail, and I'll explore this one," I said with confidence. "We'll meet back here in about ten minutes." It wasn't a great plan, but it was a plan. She hesitantly trudged down the right-hand path while I hiked into the unknown on the left. Discovering nothing of note, I went back to the split and sat on a moss-covered log to wait. I took off my new hiking boots, soaked from fording streams, to give my feet a breather. They were killing me.

Twenty minutes and still no cockney lass.

I couldn't just sit there, so I forced my sodden shoes back on, which did nothing to help my blisters. "Ruth! Bob! You down there?" A flock of noisy parrots mocked me in reply. I limped slowly down the right-hand path and rounded a bend, where I saw her sitting in the middle of the dark trail. "What're ya doin'?" I shouted.

She looked up and screamed, "Carroll! 'elp." She was trapped calf-deep in mud, frantically struggling to get free.

"If I get too close, I'm afraid I'll get stuck. That won't do either of us any good." She squirmed while I gave it some thought. "Don't struggle, it'll just make things worse. Lean over and pull yourself out."

"O've tried. Don' work."

A heavy-duty vine hung nearby. I grabbed it and pulled. It held. "We'll try this." *I hope it's stronger than the Tarzan Swing.* I swung it over and she caught it on the first try, but it slipped through her muddy fingers when I pulled. My second toss wasn't close while the third whacked her. "Don' 'it me 'ead," she snapped while grabbing it.

"Sorry. Wrap it around your wrist." I slowly tugged, and she started to inch free. "Hang on Ruth—almost there." Our fingers touched and I dragged her out. If it had been quicksand, she would've been a goner. She scraped off the worst of the mud, looking not too happy.

Two roads diverged in a yellow wood and I ... I was lost.

"Let's wait back at the intersection. Someone will realize we're missing."

Sitting on the damp log, we babbled about nothing in particular, then fell silent. Jungle chatter could be musical or terrifying, depending on circumstances. Then something sounded faintly familiar, "Onward Christian Soldiers"?

"Ruth. Do you hear that?"

"Yah, 'tis blowin'," she said.

While I tried to figure out what she meant, the foliage behind us rustled. My heart caught in my throat—a cougar? Suddenly, Bob's grinning face appeared. He chided us, "Are you two taking a break?" He'd stopped to rinse off in a waterfall.

"Nah, jus' waitin' on you," I awkwardly lied.

"You guys aren't lost, are you?" he laughed. "And what's with all the mud?" I wore my share of it after pulling Ruth out of the pit. Without another word, Bob turned down the sinkhole trail. When Ruth tried to dissuade him, he explained, "You probably didn't notice the narrow bypass. Let's get going. It'll be dark soon." She couldn't even fake a smile.

We soon came upon the grass airstrip I'd landed on previously. As dusk approached, I slowly hobbled down the runway. Children's laughter came from the direction of the mission house.

A large crowd was gathered in the dusty front yard where Kate sat on a primitive chair with Joel standing behind her. Queen Kate and Prince Joel were smiling at the inner circle of laughing children. No one made a fuss over my arrival. Folks were more interested in the tall, fair-skinned lady and her very white, very blond, blue-eyed boy.

In her element, Kate sang familiar songs while kids squealed with delight. Some of them joined her, creating a jumbled chorus of Chinentaco, Spanish, and English. Whatever the tongue, music never failed to bring joy.

"Hey, ya'll. We finally made it."

Kate glanced up, beaming. "They're so warm and friendly. Where's Ruth?"

"Covered in mud, more than me. Probably went to clean up in the river."

Kate looked puzzled.

"I'll explain later. What's wrong with you, Joel?"

"They keep touching me." As if on cue, one tyke snuck up to touch the gringo kid while his buddies giggled. Even adults couldn't resist patting his towhead. Hungry, Joel had had enough.

"At least you don't have hair on your arms—they're plucked as trophies."

"Daaad!" Joel didn't see the humor.

"Did you get any fresh bananas?" I asked. "We did."

That news fell flat; all they'd eaten was oatmeal cookies.

"Dinner time," Bob bellowed, saving me from myself. "Ann and Ruth are already at the hut, just down that lane."

As we followed Bob, a kid dashed out to touch Joel one last time before we ducked into a dark, smoke-filled hovel. A simple split-log table was piled high with food. The elderly matron had prepared a veritable feast: some kind of fowl, rice, and vegetables. Kate and Joel could be picky eaters, but not tonight. Famished, they dug in while hens and chicks pecked at scraps that fell onto the dirt floor. A rooster crowed outside; night was falling.

With a full belly, Joel was happier and resumed playing with the kids outside. Kate followed him and hummed contentedly. The crowd hushed when she began to sing. So far, our difficult trek had proved worthwhile.

"Time for bed," Bob announced. For some unknown reason the women, along with Joel, bunked indoors while the men-folk slept outside on the ground.

Kate was unhappy with the arrangement. "What do they think we're going to do?"

I didn't have an answer, but that was the custom.

Weary, I lay atop my bedroll and gazed up at the numberless stars. In the distance, I heard the low, guttural growl of a roving puma. The cooking fires would keep them away. The jungle sounds began to lull me, and I rolled over to drift asleep.

CHAPTER NINETEEN

Into the Unknown

The cocks crowed before sunrise and I awoke groggy. My feet hurt from multiple blisters that had seemingly coalesced into one big one. Pulling on damp shoes was excruciating, but nothing compared to limping through Usila's dry streets for a hearty breakfast of scrambled eggs, peppers, onions, and fire-sauce, all spread on a fresh tortilla.

"Carroll. Why don't you ride today?" Kate noticed how much pain I was in. "I had a restful night—alone. Besides, I'm saddle-sore and could use the walk."

It didn't take much to convince me, knowing I wouldn't be able to keep up on foot. "Bob said we'll split up like yesterday and meet around lunchtime. We can switch off then." I agreed, totally forgetting about Kate's newly diagnosed asthma.

I hopped astride a burro far too small for me and leaned over to kiss Kate. When the ornery beast nipped at her he stumbled, and I reflexively grabbed the saddle horn. "This animal's nuts."

Kate replied, "You're right—mean *and* clumsy." He brayed and kicked in retort.

Joel, already mounted, waved. "Bye, Mom. See ya at lunch."

For some reason, only two mounts were available: my loco burro and some weird-looking thing with hooves for Joel. Ruth wasn't happy, forced to hike a second day. I started to make a wisecrack about mud pits, but then thought better of it.

Bob and the ladies climbed aboard a sizable log raft that a ferryman poled across the Usila River. Crossing at an upstream ford, my burro stumbled and half fell in the river, which again soaked my shoes. Back on dry ground, Joel and I rode side by side and talked about last night's touchy-feely fest with the village kids.

"How're ya doing today, son?"

"I'm fine, Dad. A couple boys asked me to play this morning. One of them let me use his bow. It was small and the string felt like a rubber band."

"Elastic? I guess civilization is closing in."

Last year, from the bush plane, I'd seen heavy equipment chewing a road through the jungle, Tuxtepec to Usila. Of course, Cokes and Dos Equis had arrived several years earlier.

Humble yet picturesque homes dotted the landscape, and the rhythmic rocking of the saddle and warm sun was soothing. Suddenly, without warning, my jackass shied at a wild turkey that strutted across our path. He took off, following it through the tangled underbrush. We plowed through a stick fence, which tore at my jeans. No longer complacent I yanked the rope reins, but he was impossible to handle with only a halter. I tugged his head to the side until it almost touched my leg. When he nipped at me, it gave the turkey time to escape.

Loco, for so I named him, repeatedly tripped and staggered, slamming me against whatever tree or post was handy. When I kicked him, he bucked in reply.

"Donkeys are sure-footed," Bob had said. Not this one. He stepped erratically on the steep, boulder-strewn paths, especially when going downhill toward the river flats. It was all I could do to hang on.

Standing in an open field, a bull loomed in the near distance. Loco's ears went flat and he picked up the pace to challenge him, a duel he'd surely lose—and with me on his back. My heart pounded when he took off in a run. *I'm gonna die*, I thought. I pulled the rope until his nose touched my knee, ignoring a possible bite. That only slowed him. He not only continued to charge at a gallop, he now became quite surefooted, not tripping at all.

The bull saw us coming, lifted his head, and snorted. With his powerful hoof, he pawed the ground and sized us up, then relaxed, like he was bored. On the run, Loco kicked sideways as we passed *el toro*, who ignored the insult and resumed his lazy grazing. I breathed a sigh of relief and shouted, "Damn jackass." Joel caught up and smiled; he'd seldom heard his dad cuss.

The trail delved deeper into the jungle, leaving the quaint farms behind. The trees became massive and tall, filtering the tropical sun. We saw more wildlife on this leg of our trek: squawking parrots flew erratically while scores of lizards scampered up tree trunks and dozens of iguanas lazed high on tree limbs. To me, it was heaven on earth. I began humming, and I couldn't carry a tune.

"Dad. That's a Sunday school song."

"Really? Today's Sunday, isn't it?"

After a few hours, our guide called a halt. "Ladies here … soon, maybe." I thought he only spoke Chinentaco, and maybe a little Spanish.

Dismounting, Joel and I started to explore but my feet ached and burned. I sat down and leaned against a tree. Its enormous roots rose from the soft jungle floor like the flying buttresses of gothic cathedrals. They formed a sort of easy chair that I settled into.

In an exhausted stupor, I stared at the myriad insects carrying seeds over and around the ferns that carpeted the ground. Vines hung everywhere; I glimpsed a couple of orchids growing in the trees. Birds chirped from somewhere high in the canopy, and Joel spotted a rare macaw that talked to us. With youthful energy, he reconnoitered while my eyes grew heavy.

As I slumbered, the trekking half of our group emerged from a dark tunnel of foliage, huffing and puffing. Trudging near the back of the line, Kate was wheezing. "Whew ... long hike," she rasped between labored breaths. She gulped some water. "You would've loved it, Carroll. We crossed a swinging bridge over a high gorge. And I saw several monkeys!" Excited, she drank too fast and water spilled down her sweat-soaked shirt. She was wiped out.

"Look, Kate, I've had a decent break. You ride for the afternoon."

"But your feet ..." She tilted her head and took another long drink.

"They're fine. We'll be together from here on out and can switch off anytime." I really wanted her to ride; she didn't look good. "And go easy on the water," I said to change the subject and end the debate. "Too much too fast can make you sick."

"If you think you'll be okay."

"I'm fine." To prove it, I walked in a small circle, forcing myself not to limp.

Joel volunteered to walk with me. He'd ridden all day yesterday, and we were having a good time together. Ruth, who'd hiked both days, quickly claimed his animal. "I canna 'ike another 'ill."

Cold tortillas sufficed for lunch, and we prepared to move on. When Kate deftly mounted my loco-burro, an Indian grabbed her reins, although she was an accomplished horseman. Maybe it was because the Brit mounted from the wrong side. A guide shoved Ruth's ample backside onto the burro.

Joel and I took point, right behind the lead guide. Kate and Ruth were on their mounts, positioned in the middle of the pack animals and porters while Bob took up the rear, his sunburnt visage standing out amidst the native brown.

"Head 'em out," Bob called. Loco refused to budge. The Indian yanked on the reins, and the donkey pulled back. Kate kicked the burro, who brayed then tripped forward.

The trail soon split; one followed along the flats while the one we took climbed steeply. Kate shouted, "Carroll! My saddle's sliding off the back of this crazy thing."

"Don't worry," I hollered back. "There's no way it can come off. You'll be fine—just hang on to your crazy ass." I meant the donkey.

Kate was about thirty yards behind when I turned to take her picture. Peering through the viewfinder, I noticed Bob's faded red baseball cap bobbing in the lower background. It was a great shot, but I couldn't pause for long; we had to make Tejas before nightfall. Apparently, it was still a long way off.

I smiled at Joel. "Let's pick up the pace and beat her to the top." He grinned and started to quickly march when I heard a thump behind us, different from other jungle sounds. Curious, I turned and saw Bob running up the trail, past the porters and Ruth. He stopped to look into the heavy jungle foliage, then exclaimed something unintelligible before racing back down.

Where's Kate? I wondered. I'd just seen her through the camera lens. *And why does Bob look freaked out?* Something wasn't right.

I ran back down to where Kate had been when I took her picture. The dense undergrowth had camouflaged a precip- itous cliff along which we'd just hiked. Kate's burro, with her on it, had tripped and fallen off the edge. They punched a hole through the dark foliage. She lay sprawled at the bottom of a twenty-five foot drop-off, having landed on a pointed boulder that split her head open. Blood oozed onto the fern-covered jungle floor.

Blood drained from my face. *My wife is dead!*

From the heights, I saw her feet move ever so slightly, just a twitch or two. *No. She's alive!* I shoved through the crowd of porters and ran down to a switchback I hadn't noticed before. Unbeknownst to me, Joel followed hard on my heels.

I found Bob kneeling over my wife, talking softly into her ear. "Kate … Kate. Wake up, sweetie." He looked up at me, horror on his face. "She's losing a lot of blood, Carroll."

I sat beside her and gently laid her head on my lap. The back of her skull had burst like a daylily. I grabbed my canteen to flush the wound; warm water and blood drenched my filthy shirt and jeans. Kate's lifeblood was spilling onto me, and the only credible blood bank was days away.

My hands shook while I explored her wound. The bone was intact. Scalp wounds bled like crazy so it looked worse than it was. I folded the skin closed and applied pressure with my palm. "Someone get my duffle bag." Bob translated my demand and the bag soon appeared.

"Bob. I have several bottles of antibiotics. They're oral, but better than nothing." I opened several capsules, dumped them into my canteen and irrigated the gash with the makeshift mixture. It dawned on me how hard she must've hit; swelling on the brain became a concern.

Her eyes fluttered open. "What'd I do wrong?"

I felt relief, but also guilt. "Nothing, hon. You didn't do anything wrong. That dumb donkey just slipped."

She managed to swallow some antibiotics and the narcotics I'd brought. Kate's eyes involuntarily shut, then flickered back open. She anxiously repeated, "What'd I do wrong?"

"Nothing, you didn't do anything wrong."

"Is the donkey okay?"

"He's fine," I said, though I wanted to kill it.

"Carroll. My back's broken." Her lips quivered.

"I don't think so, sweetie … your feet and legs are moving."

"Yes it is. I'm sure of it. I don't feel anything." Fear welled in her eyes.

Having second thoughts, I loosened her jeans and pulled her shirt up. She was bruised from the small of her back down to her thighs. It was bad, but everything seemed to be working, so I continued to comfort her. "You're badly hurt, Kate. But nothing seems to be broken." I didn't share my concerns about cranial swelling.

All the while, she kept repeating the same few phrases:

"What'd I do wrong?"

"Is the donkey okay?"

"My back is broken. I can't feel my legs."

Then she came up with the clincher that made me turn away and weep.

"Can we go home now? I want to go home."

"Sure we can," I said, choking through tears. But I had no idea how to extricate her from this heaven turned hell-hole.

CHAPTER TWENTY

———

The Rescue

Although alive, Kate had lost a lot of blood and needed hospital care, but we were a two-day trek from Tuxtepec, which itself lacked advanced medical facilities.

Bob paused from praying and looked up. "It'll be okay, Carroll."

"How?" I probably sounded desperate—or maybe angry. "How will it be okay?"

"I sent a runner to Usila for help. He'll be back faster than we got here in the first place." Bob added, "Joel won't be able to keep up when they carry Kate out. He's got to go back now."

I balked at sending my young son without me, knowing now just how dangerous the jungle could be. "Don't worry," Bob encouraged. "Ann and Ruth will go along with a guide."

It made sense. I turned to Joel. "You need to return to Usila right now." I tried to be firm, but my voice cracked.

Tears trailed down his dirty face as he shook his head. "No, Dad."

"You don't want to slow down your mom's rescue, do

———

199

you?" Maybe I sounded too harsh. "We'll be along shortly," I added softly.

He finally agreed, and Ann took his hand. Wearing his Cub Scout hat, he plodded slump-shouldered into that dark, tunnel-like trail from which his mom had emerged an hour ago. As he was engulfed by the foreboding jungle, a lump formed in my throat. *Oh God. What have I done to my family?*

Bob and I settled in to wait. Hours crept by like days. Although the bleeding stopped, Kate continued to moan. Drifting in and out of consciousness, she repeatedly muttered the same lines:

"My back's broken."

"What'd I do wrong?"

"Is the burro okay?"

"I want to go home. Can we go home now?"

"Sure," I'd answered to the last one, but without roads or modern communications, how could I pull it off? Over the hours, she repeated each sentence, in exactly the same order as if for the first time, and each time I choked out the same lie. "We'll head back soon, Kate."

Obviously in pain, Kate moved her legs spastically. Bob laid hands on her in prayer, and an eerie peace enveloped the rainforest. I felt an inexplicable serenity.

A flock of birds suddenly took flight, startling me, and the Indian runner with a rescue party burst through the thick underbrush. I wondered if they'd crossed paths with Joel but didn't ask.

Several villagers cut down a few hanging vines while another chopped and limbed a medium-sized tree. They apparently planned to carry Kate by tying her hands and feet to a ten-foot pole like a fresh deer carcass.

"They've got to make a stretcher," I shouted to Bob. "There's no telling what's wrong with her back. It might be broken."

He agreed and barked orders that were quickly translated

into Chinentaco. They cut more trees and vines—no one thought to bring rope—and made a rectangular frame over which her bedroll was laid. After I gently slid her onto it, four Indians hoisted the makeshift contrivance, which bowed in the middle, and took off at a fast pace. Two of them bushwhacked shortcuts through the jungle. Thankfully, the route we took was flat and avoided cliffs.

I limped along on my badly blistered feet and soon fell behind, periodically losing sight of the rescue party. After an hour or so they stopped to adjust the crude stretcher, which allowed time for me to catch up. When they laid hands on Kate, it was the only time she stopped moaning.

I felt totally useless.

After this brief respite, the rescue team moved even faster. I simply couldn't keep up despite an adrenaline surge, and they disappeared from sight where I could no longer hear them. I struggled to pick up the pace, but it wasn't enough. Helplessness turned to panic. My wife had vanished into the depths of an unchartered rainforest, and I felt forsaken.

Following the newly bushwhacked trail, I emerged onto a main path. A couple hundred yards later it split into two equal byways. Which way to go? *I'll go right.* There was no particular logic to this.

As my protesting feet stepped off, an old guy emerged from the woods. I lowered my head to bowl past him, in no mood to negotiate the right of way, but he led a horse that completely blocked the path. As I continued toward them, they held their ground.

Wrinkled and older than dirt, he was stooped and partially toothless. A half-open dirty white shirt revealed scraggily gray chest hair, and his baggy white pants were held up by twine tied around his waist. A floppy sombrero too tired to hold the proud shape of its youth capped off the ensemble. With unshod leathered feet, he could've walked straight out of a spaghetti Western as either the bad or the ugly—certainly not the good.

I plowed ahead, planning to push the smelly old coot and his horse out of my way. For some strange reason, though, I paused, mesmerized by his bright eyes that seemed out of place. I imagined Kate's broken body reflected in them, while a grin spread across his wizened face. His fragile hand stretched out and gently took my hand, placing the hemp reins in it. *He's giving me his horse!*

Unlike the quintessential jackass, this was a fine palomino with only a rope halter and reins, no saddle or bridle. I jumped up and threw my leg over bareback. He immediately took off at a gallop without the slightest kick from me.

The whole encounter probably took only seconds. Astride the racing horse, my hope was renewed—except ... *is this even the correct trail?* I wondered.

The muscular beast sprinted as branches smacked my face. Another fork approached and my spirit sank. To take the wrong path might mean becoming irrevocably lost. I tugged, but he refused to slow down. He veered hard left without breaking stride. Two or three more times, the stallion never hesitated at a fork, instinctively knowing the way.

Despite racing at a full gallop, it seemed like an interminably long ride. Several times I was almost thrown by a quick turn but remained mounted. Suddenly, we burst into a broad boulder-strewn field. In the blinding glare of the late sun, the horse stopped dead and refused to budge no matter how much I kicked; the terrain was too treacherous for him.

I squinted and saw the Usila River coursing through a distant ravine (I assumed it was the Usila). Quickly dismounting, I handed the reins back to the old guy and made for the river, stumbling over loose rocks. It's a wonder I didn't twist an ankle.

Upon reaching the river's edge, I saw Kate being carried across midstream, the Indians wading chest-high through raging whitewater while holding her high. It was an unused shortcut. They clambered up the far bank's slippery slope, balancing Kate.

I was ready to take the plunge when stopped by a couple of Indians. The last of four river crossings, this was the trickiest. They bound three logs together as a makeshift raft onto which I scrambled. It was wildly tossed while they struggled to walk me across, refusing to let go. Without saying thank you, I scaled the bank and entered town.

It was like a ghost town; no one was around. Chickens wandered and pecked while pigs snorted and grunted. I hobbled down the main street toward voices that came from the east. Passing the last hut, I crossed a gully into an open field that was the familiar grass airstrip.

Kate lay on the stretcher beside several crates of beer under the shade of a spreading Ceiba tree. It appeared that all of Usila was gathered around that rickety bush plane Bob had tried to hire last year. The grungy pilot/drug runner had just flown several cases of Dos Equis over the mountains.

Joel stood in the shadow of the old cub's wing, talking to the pilot. When it landed, Joel realized that this might be the only way to get his mom out—quick thinking for a seven-year-old. With rudimentary Spanish learned in elementary school, Joel got *el capitán* to wait until Kate arrived. The man would fly anything for a price. A year later, Kate and I learned that Joel had fully expected her to be dead.

"I can't believe this," Bob exclaimed. "Planes never fly into Usila on Sunday!"

"You're kidding?" I fully expected to spend the night nursing Kate in a hut.

"Yep. Jus' doesn't happen." After an introspective moment, Bob shouted, "Get that door off the plane. *Rápido!*"

In a flash, the door was removed so Kate could be put onto the floor without bending her. Joel and I squeezed in beside her; again, only the pilot had a seat. He climbed aboard, fastened an antiquated, WWII leather helmet, secured vintage round goggles, and fired up the engine. Kate bounced unmercifully on the runway until airborne.

Swirling wind currents tossed us uncomfortably close to the rocky peaks. Throughout the day, I had given Kate a number of painkillers—probably too many. In the turbulence, she vomited half-digested scrambled eggs. Not happy about the smelly mess sloshing across the floor, the pilot yelled something in Spanish; he probably regretted his decision to take the gringos to Tuxtepec.

Maybe feeling a bit better, Kate asked, "Are we airborne yet?" She had no idea.

"We sure are, and headed home," I feebly said, knowing this was a half-truth.

Joel anxiously stared at a strip of duct tape on a cracked window. "Is this plane safe?"

I glanced at the fat, unshaven pilot and lied. "Sure. That guy's trained and licensed." *Maybe.* "He wouldn't go up in it if it wasn't safe, right?"

Joel shrugged, not sure what to think, and stared back out the window.

We descended toward a valley that looked as peaceful as anything in Creation, a luscious carpet of green with a sliver of silver bordered by tall, overhanging trees. A clearing appeared and we began a steep spiral. The ground raced up at a dizzying pace. At the last minute we leveled off and buzzed the runway before making a final go around.

"See the airstrip, Joel? We're back."

"Uh-huh."

The plane hit hard; Kate groaned in pain and continued to dry heave. Our pilot hopped out and walked around the still-turning propeller as I climbed out the back. He held out a filthy hand, which I heartily shook.

"Gracias ... gracias señor."

He grimaced and yanked it away, palm up; he wanted pesos.

"I don't have any money. I have to get hold of Flo." The guy understood "Flo" and stalked over to a grimy black rotary phone in the maintenance hut. He spoke briefly, hung up, sat on a stool, and rocked back against the door.

In short order, I heard the engine knock of Bob's Suburban; a dust cloud trailed it on the service road. Flo jumped out. "Why are you back here, Doc?"

"Kate's burro fell off a cliff with her on it. She's in the plane, badly injured." I glanced at the pilot as he rocked forward on the stool, suspiciously eyeballed me, and walked to the SUV.

"He needs money," Flo said. "For three passengers and something about a clean-up."

"I know, but I'm broke. All my money is somewhere between Usila and another village. I can pay you back later."

"I'll take care of it." Flo counted out pesos, most of what she had. Missionaries were chronically strapped for cash. The pilot clenched the bills in his sweaty palm and stalked away, disappearing into the maintenance shed/watering hole where booze awaited.

Flo quickly removed the Suburban's jump seat so Kate could recline flat for the drive into town. After Joel and I hopped into the back with Kate, Flo floored it, speeding toward a clinic she normally dealt with.

Dr. Peutlino's medical facility was a single-story, cinder brick building whose windows lacked glass or screens. Its warped and cracked wooden doors were sorely in need of paint and locks. Concrete peeked through the worn linoleum floor.

The doorway around back didn't have a door, only a rotting jamb with rusty hinges that recalled a prouder past. It opened onto a manure-covered barnyard sporting several farm animals. Chickens strutted into the clinic at will. A large pig periodically poked his nose inside and snorted. Lizards scurried across the crumbling plaster walls.

The four patient rooms each had two steel beds with thin lumpy mattresses, ratty blankets, and stained sheets. The pillows shed what little stuffing was left in them. Dented metal cabinets on wheels that contained medical supplies doubled as end tables, but with no lamps.

Despite the sad-looking scene, the nurses wore clean, albeit old, uniforms that sported the classic white cap pinned to a bun. They fawned over Kate, their ivory smiles accentuated by flawless brown faces and genuine compassion. She would receive the best care possible in this destitute corner of the world.

Dusk was turning to night when Dr. Peutlino's associate— Dr. P wasn't in town—arrived to irrigate and suture Kate's head wound. I was relieved to see his instruments came from a sealed autoclave bag, but the prepackaged sutures resembled rope. *Hemp?* After closing the gash, he started IV antibiotics and steroids.

Flo referred to the young doc as *el Chen*, the Chinaman. I never caught his real name. He was third-generation Mexican and second-generation physician. His physiognomy was similar to that of the locals, but his skin tone was noticeably different. Both he and Dr. Peutlino were meticulous and caring; neither would accept payment.

All the while, Kate became ever more aware of her surroundings, focusing on a ceiling fan that wobbled. "Great! I survive, only to be decapitated by that," she muttered.

Joel and I spent the night in the clinic. Two lizards decided to mate in Kate's room, which briefly gave Joel something to watch since there was no TV. In the morning, we awoke to car horns, crowing roosters, and blaring music. It hadn't been a nightmare.

Dr. Peutlino examined Kate early that morning and

expressed concern about her incredibly discolored back and the fact that she couldn't stand. He didn't have an X-ray machine, so he packed us off in an ancient Datsun station wagon that proudly displayed *Ambulancia* on the front, hand-painted in reverse. The back of the wagon felt like a sauna despite a tiny oscillating fan, and the driver seemed to aim for every pothole.

It was too painful for Kate to lie on her back. The techs asked her to stand, but she couldn't without support. One of them demonstrated how I could hold her up by wrapping my arms around her waist.

"But aren't you also getting my skeleton in this radiograph?" I asked.

"*Qué?*"

After two exposures, someone finally figured that out and mimed that I should jump away at the last second. When I did, she immediately collapsed and slammed face down onto the table. She screamed in agony, and I got angry.

"No more X-rays." I made a cut sign across my throat. "Where's that crappy ambulance?"

It was parked illegally on the curb. I was about to hop inside when a technician ran out of the clinic with some dark, grainy films. "Nothing broke." Maybe they were looking at my bones.

Dr. Peutlino called a neurosurgeon in Veracruz who took an entire day off to travel to Tuxtepec to help us—strangers to him. He upped Kate's steroids to forestall any potential swelling of the brain. Again, payment was refused (though I did get a bill from radiology).

While Kate recuperated, she played circular solitaire in bed. I'd never heard of it and thought she was hallucinating. Intrigued, the nurses gathered around her bedside to watch. They sang to her in Spanish while Kate tried to join in in English. They had a lot of laughs.

Alert after a few days, Kate asked to be moved to the mission compound where the young girls—one-time drug addicts, alcoholics, and prostitutes—doted on her.

No longer tethered to an IV, Kate needed shots twice daily to taper off the steroids. Dr. P demonstrated how to administer them in her gluteus maximus.

Now I've given lots of shots to horses over the years—to distract the animal, I would punch its fleshy shoulder, then quickly sink the needle to the hilt while pushing the plunger. Before the animal knew what I was up to, it was done. This method works great on half-ton horses ... but not on your wife.

Disadvantaged by a poorly timed flashback, I slugged Kate's black and blue buttocks and stabbed. She howled, as much in anger as in pain. I was mortified; it was only the second time she'd screamed throughout the whole ordeal. After the series was finished, I only administered shots in her mouth.

After all the loving care Kate received, she was ready to head home, and so were Joel and I. Bob drove as gingerly as he could over the harrowing road to Veracruz. At the airport, attendants maneuvered Kate through the terminal in a wheelchair with one horribly wobbly wheel.

On the tarmac at the bottom of the metal stairs, I stared up at the plane. *How are we going to get her up that?* I wondered. Two attendants suddenly pushed by me and carried her up the steps, wheelchair and all. As the chair wouldn't fit in the aisle, I helped her stand, but unable to lift her feet, she twisted them back and forth to scoot down the aisle. Not one first-class passenger offered her a seat as she slowly, and painfully, shuffled past. This was repeated on all three flights. With open briefcases and half-drained cocktails, they offered sympathy, but no help.

"She can't even lift her feet, poor thing."

"They should've given her the bulkhead. More room."

"I know a good lawyer who'll sue the pants off that Indian," declared one loudmouth.

Place the blame, look compassionate, but don't be inconvenienced. It was so different from the generosity shown by destitute Indians. After the last agonizing flight, we finally landed at Dulles International. "Take me home, Carroll. I want to sleep in my own bed."

"Sure. Whatever you want," I assured her.

I'd arranged for Natalia to pick us up at the airport. She took us straight to Gloyd and helped me carry Kate into our house using an office stool as a wheelchair.

Kate didn't call her parents until the following day when she settled in, not wanting to alarm them after having lost her only sister, Annette, to a sniper's bullet.

I called our family physician. When he came to the house, I feebly smiled as he walked into the bedroom. "So whaddaya think, Max?"

He looked incredulous. "She needs to be hospitalized. This could be spinal cord." Then he added, "You're a piece of work, Carroll" while reaching for the phone. A half-hour later we got her into my car. His one concession was not to call an ambulance.

Although the hospital was clean and sterile with no farm animals poking about, it was cold and impersonal, except for a kind lady wearing a cross and an infectious grin who listened to Kate's story.

"Honey. You're doing the Lord's work, but now's the time to take care of yourself."

She was the only nurse who showed compassion.

When she started to remove the sutures from Kate's scalp, she said, "What's this stuff? Feels like wire." I wanted to tell her it was probably hemp, but didn't.

After a few days and numerous CT scans, Kate returned home. Her bilaterally broken pelvis had shifted beyond surgical intervention, and her shattered sacrum had to heal on its own. She was bedridden for almost four months. Time was the only cure for her concussion and nerve damage.

All the while, the people of Gloyd and our church turned out in droves to help. More meals arrived at our doorstep than my family could eat in a year. One lady picked up our laundry and returned it, folded and ironed. Many did mundane housework. The horses, dogs, cats, rabbit, and fish were well fed and well groomed. A landscaping crew weeded and mulched the flowerbeds. When Tara couldn't do it, volunteers drove Joel to Cub Scouts, violin practice, T-ball, and youth group. A Good Samaritan took Kate's place at my reception desk. She refused to be paid.

America is truly a land of selfless givers.

The bruise so prominent on Kate's backside took the better part of a year to fade. And although life eventually returned to a new normal, she continued to have a hard time physically, especially sitting for long car rides. But after a time, she began to manage the office again, head up the women's ministry, and nurse Joel after his own brush with death (see book three).

While Kate has fond memories of all who aided her recovery, the only memory she has of the actual fall was the feeling that a giant hand had let her down slowly to soften the landing, and one glimpse of a whitewater crossing when she wondered why they wouldn't lower her into the cool water. She can't, however, stomach scrambled eggs, her last meal before upchucking them inside the drug-runner's airplane.

Joel survived the nightmare with no physical scars, but the psychological ones run deep.

Several years later, with advances in surgical technique, Kate had an operation that was so successful she could even horseback ride again—not hell-bent through the woods like we used to do, but still have fun. She's even participated in a couple of foreign missions, but never to a remote jungle, and nothing that involved donkeys or cliffs. "Jackasses kill more people than cars," she contends.

One day while still bedridden, she overheard me yelling and slamming down the phone.

"Who was that, Carroll?"

"Some Hollywood guy wants to do your story. I told him to forget it, but he keeps calling." Preoccupied with taking care of her and Joel, I had repeatedly refused to do a TV short on her adventure.

Her eyes brightened. "You're kidding? They want to film us? We get to be on TV? You call them right back and say we'd be happy to do it."

We eventually made it to the small screen, but that's another story.

During times of quiet reflection, my mind would replay the events of that terrible day. After a couple years, I had a revelation. Whenever telling the story, I always included the old guy who loaned me, a complete stranger, his horse. "Imagine tossing your car keys to someone you don't know and asking him to return it at his convenience," I would say. "And I never said 'thanks' when I returned it." I'd always felt bad about not showing any gratitude.

Though our encounter was brief, I saw him vividly in my mind's eye: he wasn't even sweating when he took the reins back, nor was he breathing hard. He simply grinned with a warmth that seemed to say, *everything's gonna be okay*. He wore the same pajama outfit of the ancient peasants, not like what the other men wore, and had the same missing teeth that only a dentist would notice.

I had always been caught up in the story itself and failed to question how that old codger kept up with a galloping horse.

The truth is that he couldn't have. Carl Lewis couldn't even run that fast. A chill ran up my spine when I realized who he was, and most likely the horse.

Are they not all ministering spirits, sent forth to minister for them who shall be heirs of salvation?

I've let the facts speak for themselves.

In the end, my earthly angel has always been Kate, my loving wife. She consistently ministered to me, and no one else in this life on earth has ever meant as much.

EPILOGUE

While Kate slowly recovered, I found it incredibly uplifting that neighbors, parents at Joel's elementary school, friends, church members, and Kate's Community Bible Study pitched in when we desperately needed help. I never had to ask; folks just knew what we needed at any given time.

For instance, I didn't know the lady who came to take our laundry and change our sheets every week, but she was a godsend, returning it all pressed and folded. Once Kate was no longer confined to bed and able to resume light housework, this laundress angel moved on to help another family in need. I later found out that she wasn't just some goody-two-shoes with nothing better to do; she had a Master's in Electrical Engineering and was a bigwig at Lockheed-Martin.

Everyone asked, "Did the donkey live?" Yes, but if I'd had any say in the matter, he wouldn't have.

Kate felt that her guardian angel must've been a cousin to Clarence, the misfit seraph in the movie, *It's a Wonderful Life.* "Only," she says, "my angel caught the mule instead of me."

Life eventually returned to the abnormal normal.

In light of everything, it truly is a wonderful life.

STAY TUNED

─────────────

My next book, *And Nothing but the Tooth*, is due out in 2017 and continues the Tooth Is Stranger Than Fiction series with more stories from the farm, the office, medical missions, and my past on Nealy Ridge, which may reveal a little more about my childhood than I would've ever wanted to tell my own kids when they were growing up. But they're pretty funny.

ACKNOWLEDGMENTS

My parents and in-laws, though deceased, richly contributed to the stories in this book, and I'm thankful for their fine influence and comedic outlook in my life. They'll never know how much I appreciate them.

My life would be incomplete without my children, Tara, Russell, and Joel, for who they were and who they have become. It's been a roller-coaster ride with them as well as in life in general. The road is continuous and ever-changing, which makes it all the more interesting.

My wife Kate ran the first edit of this book and has been instrumental in seeing it to completion. Thank you for being so patient with me while I secluded myself. I wasn't hiding ... really.

Michael Garrett, who was Stephen King's first editor, was my first editor as well. I'm grateful to him for getting me on track and that he agreed to help me.

The Academy of General dentistry published shortened versions of a few stories, which gave me invaluable feedback from those readers.

Stacey Aaronson, my primary editor, designer, and publishing agent, has been a wealth of information and guidance. There's no way I could have accomplished this without her. Working with her has been fun, which made all the work and hours worthwhile and fulfilling.

My proofreaders have helped immensely with cleaning up not only several typos and other mistakes, but also in keeping a particular story flowing when the narrative might have otherwise become confusing. Thanks to Karen Rhea, Silvia Paulichen, Katrina Dzyak, Jeff Jones and, of course, Stacey Aaronson.

Thanks to everyone who has appeared in these stories whether they wanted to or not. I've changed names to protect the innocent, and maybe guard against the guilty. Life wouldn't have been the same without you and I'm in your debt.

ABOUT THE AUTHOR

DR. CARROLL JAMES is the author of *I Swear to Tell the Tooth* and a graduate of Gettysburg College, receiving his doctorate from the Farleigh-Dickenson University College of Dentistry in 1975. For two years, he practiced as an Associate in Rockville, MD, before establishing a private practice near Bethesda. After fifteen years in private practice, he began a satellite practice in Pyleton, MD (a fictional town). When that venture was unexpectedly interrupted, he purchased a home in the nearby rural town of Gloyd (also fictional) in which he established another satellite practice. That office grew exponentially and after another ten years, he moved from Rockville altogether and now enjoys treating patients in Gloyd.

Over the course of his career he has contributed articles to health columns, been published in the *CMDS Journal*, edited a monthly newsletter, lectured to medical students, written a blog, and contributed to the Academy of General Dentistry journal *Impact*. In addition, he and his family were featured in a human interest TV documentary about his wife's almost-fatal adventure in the jungles of southern Mexico.

As a child, Dr. James spent summers at his maternal grand-parent's primitive home in the rugged Appalachian heartland of southwest Virginia. This experience forged his passion for serving impoverished peoples throughout the far reaches of the world.

Blessed with three children and four live-wire grand-children, Carroll and his wife, Kate, continue to maintain their valued practice in their rural home.

CPSIA information can be obtained
at www.ICGtesting.com
Printed in the USA
BVOW04s2135220517
484889BV00001B/45/P